# LIFE

A book of short stories and poems

By Brandalyn Gill

ISBN-10: 0982909500

ISBN-13: 9780982909508

Library of Congress Control Number: 2010912112

To my father, because he never gave up
To my Grannie, my Aunt T, and my Aunt D because
they are my heart
To HOH Fellowship for giving me a start
To my God family, my Grandpa Reginald and the rest
of my loved ones, because I love you all dearly

Dear Reader,

I have compiled this book of stories and poems, all of which I have written from the heart, simply because I am perfectly certain that all living today know that life is the most trying, beautiful, exciting, relentless, horrible, magnificent, wonderful blessing from God. I sincerely hope that this book gives all that read it something to relate to, something to celebrate, something to cry about, something to smile about, something to be proud of, something more to think about.......life.

Yours Truly,

"Brandy"

# Contents

Poems:

Part I – Just Life

Part II – Love

Part III – Lessons

## Short Stories:

"Upon the very moment you stop learning, you stop living..."

Brandalyn Gill

# Poems

Poems for the heart, soul, and mind

# Part One
## Just life...

"...live as if you'll die today."

James Dean

## Intent to Live

Life: an open book of pages that never stop turning
A glimpse of a fairy tale, yearning

You watch every day go by as the pendulum in a clock
Like the sun, the moon, the sand, the air, tick-tock

Trying to make decisions to mold the sculpture right
Like the green in the scenery and the blink of an eye

To cry, to laugh, to smile, to hurt
To hug, to kiss, to tell, to flirt

You try and fail and yet prevail
You hope and pray and ascertain
You breathe and speak its majestic name

What doesn't kill you makes you stronger
If you fail to dream, you live no longer

An abstract painting of colors so bright
The stars and sky of a winter night

An education - school and more
Your tasks of benevolence upon the floor

The adjacent way to love and hate
The many ways to contemplate

*Poems about Life*

We all succeed to do this deed
The intent to live, like an honorable steed

Cross the meadow to the open plain
Through the gates and find you're sane

It takes a lot to give, to give
This thing I call intent to live

*Poems about Life*

<u>Eternity</u>

Pebbles skipping across a barren lake in mid-winter
Trees swaying with the summer breeze
The delicate scent of a lily spreading its aroma throughout
The touch of a delicate hand to wake you every morning
The smell of the fresh-brewed coffee to drink
The short, but relaxing car ride through town
The light and shine a small smile brings to a room
A small animal running through the forest at the peak of dawn
The wind blowing through the meadow
Children in the park, jovial and gay-
With soft hands and cheeks
A candle that never really burns out
The gates of the heavens and the cellar to hell
Eternity is it all; Eternity it will always be…

## The Valley of Beauty

Cerulean seas intertwined into oceans that spread across the vast land -
Land of bright green pastures that sweep across the earth as a quilt of a
thousand stories
Trot across, they do, the creatures of the land
All with specific abilities and individual personality
From the Sahara of Africa to the mountain peaks of the Rockies
A creation so divine and so unique, no mind that dwells here could
think of
A golden sun to remind the tenants of the land of their creator
And a pearl white moon to show the grace the creator has for His
creation
The trees like green doors to new worlds and the ground like a path to
lead you back again
Beautiful, do they stand
Beautiful, will they always
This wonderment and marvel to every direction
Is pure from the outskirts of the Texan plain to the calm and cool
beaches of the California coast
The rain, the snow, the sleet, the hail - all fall to show a sign
All fall to show this land we have is yours as it is mine
From the canopies of the Brazilian rainforests
To the heated grounds of the Australian Outback
The winds of the Kansas climate to the frigid air of Mount Everest
From a giving heart to a receiving hand-
God gave us this place to forever remain: The Valley of Beauty

## To Be a Woman

They bear, inside them, the children of tomorrow
They carry the weight of their trepidation, broadly on their shoulders
They make important decisions from day to day, hoping only to be right
They are the Eve of Eden and life itself, plentiful in all their wealth -
Not the wealth of money, you see, but love and beauty
They speed through life with emotions so mixed and not decided
Whether to find their long lost Adam - to seek love, requited
With slender hips and crimson lips, they prance their way through
life...
Never sure what troubles the following day will carry along or what is
next to seek
Simply taking life by the day or maybe by the week
They've come so far from things simply untold
With faith and hope being all they have to hold
From the business world to the streets of the slums
And the equality issue seemed so glum
If they wore pants, if they wore a skirt -
Or plaid or a long-sleeve shirt
They'll stand tall and ambivalent and never lose their pride
Leaving nothing of themselves to be left to hide
From the beginning of time to the end and eternity
To be a woman, to be a woman...

## Breathe

Breathe
Let the solemn breath of life glide across your face
Take the time to sit and simply meditate
Breathe
Walk across a green sea of serenity
Welcome in a friend to your home of hospitality
Breathe
Let go of all your past secrets far away
Let your train ticket expire under blank terms of delay
Breathe
Let your bath water flow unto the tile floor
Spend all your riches until there simply is no more
Breathe
Read a novel that takes you to another place
Let a smile lighten up your pretty face
Breathe
Know that you only have one life to live
Know that tears are sometimes all your soul has to give
Breathe
Speak your heart and know that what it says is never wrong
For it beholds the truth to life's most beautiful song
Breathe
Step back and watch all the cars pass you by
Never be afraid and never stop asking why
Breathe
Stay tranquil and let your guardian angel take a break
No long be afraid; no longer have your hands shake
Breathe

10

Stay up late, watch the stars quickly arrive
Live your life day to day to quickly strive
Breathe
God gave you breath, so breathe until your heart beats no more
Sometimes life moves so fast, like pebbles on a barren shore
Have the want to step back and just...
Breathe

## Heaven on Earth

Green trees with dark-colored leaves
Blue fish, filling the dark-colored seas
Winds twirling like a night's swift breeze
Small daisies in a meadow swinging with ease
Small children in the park, begging you please
Sitting on a porch on a moonlit night
Safe from wars and horror-filled fights
Thinking about life; is it really right?
Watching the stars while a white fire-fly catches your eye
Poke a needle in your skin; does it really hurt?
This is what I call it; I call it heaven on earth

## Safe from the World

Down under my shadows
Past all the dark wonders
Curled up inside a nook, a girl sits and ponders
In that nook, she holds the key to life
Through thick gusts, laws and rights
She sits there all wrapped up, nice and tight
And wonders what others dream at night
Below the meadow
Through the forest
In a land of the poorest,
Lies a soul taken forever, you'll see:
Safe from the world, that's what she'll be

**Part Two**
Love

"It is strange how often a heart must be broken before the years can make it wise"

Sara Teasdale


"The greater capacity to love, the greater your capacity to feel the pain"

Jennifer Aniston

## Unconditional Love

You can say you love someone and not mean the words
While they begin to think of what they thought they heard
For whom it may concern, love is not to be taken lightly
It is like no other phrase – not kind of, sort of, or slightly
We tend to take advantage of what it really means,
As we utilize it frivolously and take it for what it seems
But, I wonder if any have stopped to think of what it is
Is it really just a hug, one decent phone call a week, and a kiss?
It truly amuses me how people abuse this beautiful word to
death
Saying it on every opportunity like taking a breath
Even some who think they understand, do not know the truth-
The real connotation behind the phrase "I love you"
It is surely not just kisses when you see your fiancée
Or flowers and candy on another man's holiday
Love should never be confused with doing things for selfish
pleasures
And certainly not picking up the phone, when it suits *you* better
It's not coming by the office when you want company for lunch
Nor is it calling her at six a.m. because *you* see her for brunch
Love is not going anywhere with him because you don't want to
do it alone
Neither is it showing affection only when you want it to be
shown
What a pity it would be to believe that he only cooks her dinner
to get in her pants
Or that in front of his friends, he refuses to hold hands

# Poems about Love

It's simply atrocious when he's bedridden, so she decides to leave his side-
Proving that on their wedding day, at the altar, she lied
I know that love is not for those that only think of themselves
It is not for those men who cannot put their long nights of clubbing on the shelves
The truth is that love is a tricky situation -
That requires attention, time, and patience
You are not in love if you do not pick up when she calls your phone
Because she just wanted to hear your voice, but all she got was a dial tone
Love is calling him for dinner just to see his face
And not gazing at other women in that public place
This emotion can only be true if you're only satisfied in his arms
And if you do the little things just to see her charm
If you were in love, you would do for him on the days you think you can't
And no matter where you are, you would always hold her hand
You would hold him close while he cried and you were late for a meeting
And stay by his side in that hospital just to hear his heart beating
There would be calls early in the morning just to say hey
As well as flowers, chocolates, and kisses on any given day
You see, true love is unselfish, unlimited, and lasts forever
Not just when it's shining, but through the bad weather
True love is when both sides feel the same and are equally sacrificial
And when he and she are always there when needed, it becomes unconditional

*Poems about Love*

## What I Wanted You to Know (A Letter to My Last Love)

Dear Grace,

I died today, so I can only watch from above.
Unfortunately, that does not mean that I cannot love.
Of course, I thought of you when I left the house today.
Last night, I did the same thing, as I wondered if you were okay.
After our big fight a few days ago, I did not know if we were still friends.

I'm sure I said some things I could not easily mend.
Surely you were upset, because you didn't pick up when my name was on your phone. But what you didn't know was, without you for only minutes, I felt alone. You slammed the door in my face before I could tell you what I really meant. Or that every single day I see your face, I'm like an email: sent.

Certainly, you had no idea that being your best friend was never enough for me...Only because I knew deep down inside, it wasn't all we could be. But, we've known each other since childhood, and I've never told you my emotions have been everywhere. So, I knew you couldn't possible know that I even adore the smell of your hair. What a coward I was to never stick up for you when your boyfriends broke your heart. Because I was too busy saying "I told you so" - that really tore you apart. I should have come to see you, when you never returned my call, but I was too occupied with being proud and taking a fall.

## Poems about Love

I suppose it is true that you don't know what you've got until it's gone. Truth is, I did, only it took me too long. Actually, when my car crashed into the other this morning, I still loved you as I have all this time and I've watched us both grow. My love for you was the very last thing on my mind - because that was the last thing, of all things, that I wanted you to know...

Sam

## Butterflies

When I see you, I feel a smile on my face
Doesn't matter where we are; it could be any place
Even the way you walk is intoxicating to me
And you make me wonder if we are meant to be
I absolutely adore the way you talk and how you say my name
So when I think about it all day, you're to blame
As you hold my hand, I drift to another land
And I wish I could stay there, just as long as I can
How you make me feel this way, it is truly hard to tell
Because I love the way you dress and the sweet way that you
smell
If you hold me, I go crazy and lose all sense of control
So, I'll never ask you to leave; I'll never let you go
I truly hope you feel the same, as there's passion in my eyes
And my heart aches when we're not together; you give me
butterflies

*Poems about Love*

## The Truth Is...

To tell you how I feel is harder than it seems.
I am stumbling to a fall – no balance on this beam.
Your looks are captivating and your smile brings me chills.
To be under your spell is quite a task to reveal.
I act like you don't exist to see how long you'll last-
Pretending to take things slowly, when they should be taken fast.
While I hide what I feel inside, I know nothing will prevail-
When the truth is that I love you and it's so hard for me to tell.

It bothers me that you admire me and you almost refuse to let me know,
Because your face is simply handsome to everyone you show.
There lies a fire inside of me with desire to call you mine -
Wishing to let the flames escape, not wasting any time.
My emotions seem to be trapped, when your presence I endure
But you are always on my mind as I depart from you, for sure.
The things I feel may not be visible to you and are hidden by my shell,
But the truth is that I love you and it's so hard for me to tell.

I believe you are more than you believe yourself to be
And if we spent more time together, I would be proud to help you see.
I love your subtle touches and the way you say my name.
The only thing I'd hope for is for you to feel the same.
I deeply believe in courage and letting my feelings be revealed,
So just because I am shy does not mean I cannot feel.
I'm so through with keeping this secret, because it's making me want to yell.
When the truth is that I love you and now there's nothing left to tell.

## Falling Away from You

On fading love...

After struggling with you for so long, I just want to give up the fight
Although, I am not saying this out of anger, nor out of spite
We've simply grown apart and it's not meant to be
You're blinded by fallacies and I don't care to make you see
You have all these misconceptions as to who I really am,
But you do not take the time to acknowledge my glam
I cannot say I really blame you, because you've been through quite a bit
- this is true
But that is simply not an excuse and that is why we're through
I will love you all my life, but our relationship has dissipated
That is the only alternative I have, other than you being hated
With you, I cannot blossom into the beautiful person I was meant to be
Our relationship postpones that process and hopefully you get the hint
from me
I have no intentions of seeming cruel but I am sure you understand –
That it is time for me to grow, leave, and drop your hand
I don't know what has caused this or where it all has gone wrong
But I want a wonderful melody called a life, not this sad song
I am tired of the tears and being a burden as you believe what is not
true
It is a tragedy to say but I've fallen away from you

## Separated
On troubled love...

I can reach out to touch you but you are still so far.
It seems as if everyone's duty is to keep us apart.
Our love is strong but, against this evil, it is so weak -
Although, it is heavily guarded in a place that is not easily breached.
You are one of the best things to happen to me but sometimes you seem to drift away,
As I struggle to catch you, on the very worst days.
True love has always been burdened by the tribulations of life
But it still hurts when I cannot see you so this cannot be right.
Life is not fair but shouldn't two be allowed to be one...
And not driven apart or troubled by everything and everyone.
Maybe we'll have to fight for what we believe is ours -
For every kiss, hug, and moment with all of our power.
Yes, it would not be worth it if our time together wasn't grated
But that does not help my tears at night, all because we're separated.

# Part Three
Lessons

"Knowing is not enough; we must apply. Willing is not enough; we must do"

Johann Wolfgang von Goethe

"All wish to possess knowledge, but few, comparatively speaking, are willing to pay the price."

Juvenal

" God allows us to experience the low points of life in order to teach us lessons we could not learn in any other way. The way we learn those lessons is not to deny the feelings but to find the meanings underlying them."

Stanley Lindhquist

## Let the Rain Fall
On strength...

All the showers can pour down and tear down all they may
They can wash away the good and chase away the day
Let them wreak havoc in my life and ruin all I stand for
I want the rain to trickle down and then begin to pour
The tidal waves shall demolish all that's positive and catch me
unprepared
As they try to rob me of my happiness because I would not care
I have my umbrella and my galoshes are close by
I know God is there and He will hear my cry
No thunderstorm will ruin my faith and cloud my goals in life
Especially not that easily – not with one simple try
Surely, I will stand strong and I will have the gall...
To stand up to the storm; let the rain fall.

## Pretty Little Rich Girl
On REAL life...

Pretty little rich girl, any moment everything can change
A storm could blow through and tear down your estate
Your cars would be demolished, as your jewelry floats in the stream
While your shoes would be ground to a pulp and your pretty clothes into cream.
All the paintings on the wall would float away and your pretty dog would be dead
Along with all the pretty furs you put on your head
Every diamond would fall to the floor and blow away to Never Land
And your pretty house would be gone, like footprints in the sand
You precious little rich girl, you would be poor and have nothing to show
All the material things you stood for would be buried in the snow
There wouldn't be enough insurance to cover everything *you* had
And you would have no more money, because neither would your dad
You've never worked a day in your life and you've been fed with a silver spoon
You would have to fend for yourself all too soon
You would not be prepared for the dreary game of life
And you would end up like your poor brother and his poor wife
You have looked down on them for years, because your father kicked them out

But your laughter would be no more, as you would sit to pout
You see, pretty little rich girl, you're a spoiled little brat
With your expensive custom dresses and your overbearing hats
As you sit on your golden throne, you know nothing of real life –
Of what it's like without maids, butlers, and private jet flights
I hope, little princess, you will drop your tiara and break your little glass shoe
Maybe then, pretty little rich girl, you will get a clue

## Relapse
On foresight....

Many mistakes one makes are inevitably regrettable
Many times you will try to escape them, but they will certainly
get the best of you
We tend to forget that the hands of a clock only go one way
And the things we do now will be remembered another day
If you get drunk now, you'll have a hangover soon
If you smoke pot, it will surely catch up to you
Go ahead and deceive and lie, because karma is a bastard
And if you keep killing people, you are going to die faster
My father always told me that your actions define you as an
individual
So if you have a conscience, you will soon get bad visuals
Orgasms only last a few minutes, but giving birth hurts and
children last a lifetime
As a matter of fact, another six unwanted babies were born by the
time I wrote this rhyme.
You could cock a gun in a minute
But being on death row is difficult to avoid,
Even with character witnesses
So keep drinking, killing, stealing, lying, hurting others, being
stupid, wasting your life, doing nothing...
Hopefully one day, you'll wake up and smell the coffee and
perhaps -
Have a relapse...

*Poems of Lessons*

### I Thank God
On thankfulness…..


I thank the Lord wholeheartedly for the things that He has done -
For the things that make me, me-
For the person I have become
I thank him for the rainy days and all the showers I've endured
As well as for my sick days and for the body he has cured
I thank my Father for excusing all my faults -
For my body, mind, and spirit, I can do nothing but exalt
God is my only true friend and I thank him for his time
I pray he stays with me all my life, my hand in his and his in
mine

*Poems of Lessons*

## Together
On unity...

Let us join our hands in prayer for all the years we were at war -
For the constant days of battles from China to the American
shores
We shall salvage the damage done to our beloved human race
As we bring smiles to each young and innocent face
How divided our nations have become – how shattered is the
dream...
To bring every country closer, far closer than they seem
The love has been forgotten, while trust has been set aside
This world has become sickly and she is destined to die
Fire is in men's hearts on each hemisphere
All that is left in children is their undying and restless fear
Shamelessly days go by, as we have yet to join hands
As one entire people, separated not even by desert sands
Divided we have become through brutality and hate
By terror, heartache, bitterness, and many worthless debates
Crudeness and severity describe the actions of one land to
another
Consequently, dimming the love of one person towards his
brother
We have found countless reasons to continue all our fights
While the women and young ones can no longer sleep at night
The earth, she cries, as we can no longer get along
Continue on one accord and sing the chorus of one song
Various colors of skin have shielded people within
Separating the world into different universes - an act so grim
We should unite and create a beautiful circle of love

*Poems of Lessons*

Making the Lord a satisfied Parent, as he sits up above
We have managed to disappoint him enough, as we have created
our own terrible weather
I pray we come to our senses, realize we need each other, and
just...come together

## Courage

What if time ran out and you had no chance to say your last words?
And the things that you thought never were heard?
As the issues that you failed to agree with were never resolved
Because you didn't speak your mind and the problem failed to be solved
Now, if life was a challenge and one should never be discouraged
You should seriously consider being a man or woman of courage

*Poems of Lessons*

## A Letter to Hate

You have lied to this world for years and split us all apart
As you are now instilled, frozen, and planted in all of our hearts
What a pity it has been to watch you divide all of our nations
With your false truths, horrible effects, and disastrous
implications
You have single-handedly caused the deaths of hundreds of
thousands
Using religion as a tool to separate us; how could we have
allowed this?
Cunningly, you have cheated our best politicians into doing
poorly
Until there is almost no one to follow – not a soul to give the
glory
This world is disastrously divided, all in your shameful name
All the while, many have been tricked into playing your never-
ending game
No country can truly trust another because of what you have
done
Certainly, you are conniving and deceitful to everyone
We are made to believe that you are the answer to our prayers
As you have sneaked your way into all our worldly affairs
Soldiers lie breathless on the ground with no blood in their
veins,
Across this earth, on various countries' plains
All because of your influence and the damage you have caused -
For all you have destroyed, incessantly without a single pause
Your teachings are to raise the dagger when an issue is difficult to
solve

## Poems of Lessons

Instead of discussing the world's problems to surely be dissolved
I know you are the cause of all the pain in this place -
Of every tear drop freshly fallen from every saddened face
You have taken fathers from their children and compassion from
many hearts
Bamboozling many and conquering most as if it was an art
You ought to take a day off so that the peace can shine through
Because, with more love in our hearts, we would never need you

## A Tulip in the Wind
On discretion over actions...

A tulip fell onto the ground
And drifted far away
The wind carried it around
In that spot, it did not stay

The tulip traveled far and wide
Across grassy paths
It was not hidden – it will never hide
This flower, one shall have

It will pass on and travel long-
For as long as one can dream
Because most things may not be wrong-
At least, that is not how they seem

## Mind Games
On honesty......

What if you saw me from across the room, but didn't know what
to say?
Because my red dress seemed to burn right through your shades...
Would you come my way and sweetly greet me?
Or would you stay grinning in your seat, as you turn your head,
so I can't see?
What if I flipped my hair back and crossed my legs in my chair?
How would you ignore that and make it seem like you don't care?
I feel like chatting with the guy next to me, but I see you looking
out of the corner of your eye
I could see you clench your fist and then I wonder why
Would you be jealous if I slipped him my number and told him
to call that night?
I could imagine you just watching my lips closely and imagining
holding me tight
I think I would lick my lips and then gaze at you for a little while
And afterwards I would look away like a little child
Do you think you would lose control and come to get me?
What If I stood up and left because that's how it would be
You would probably sit by your friends and realize what I was all
about
But you wouldn't hesitate to make me wait longer-
To make me hunger for you more
Because you'd think I'd be waiting for you, since you were so
sure

Sooner or later, you would get the nerve to run out to the
elevator and catch me before I leave
But you would chase me to no avail; I would be way out of the
building and down the street
I can see you hanging your head in shame, for you wanted me but
you *acted* as if the feelings weren't there
So you'd mosey up the steps back to your waiting room chair
Thinking of my beautiful face and body to match,
You'd notice the dude I spoke to and the card in his lap
You'll probably walk across the room, thinking of how to ask
him for this huge request
But before you can think of an excuse, he'll hand you the card, as
you feel blessed
I know you would dial the number and every ring would make
your heart beat faster
If a silky smooth voice answered, you'd feel out of control,
On your body, a great feeling would take its toll
You would find a way to say hello and the sexy voice would
answer back
"I knew you thought I was sexy, but you didn't come over, so I
left, since you acted like that,
But I left my number for you 'cause it wasn't you to blame;
I figured it's only a guy's nature to play mind games

## <u>Stronger</u>

I wonder if it makes one weak, because one cries...
Even if in your tears, the real truth lies
For all it may concern, sometimes there is nothing left of some to
spare
As the pain begins to show and one can hardly care
Upon the times that there is nothing left to feel, while your heart
crumbles in your chest
During the moments that you tried to persevere but second-
guessed your best
Unsure of what I should write next, I'll say that it's difficult to
stand on your feet, after being pushed down
Or to put on your best smile to shield your gloomy frown
When it feels as if weights are kneeling upon your heart
Or all senses of hope are simply torn apart
Gradually, the hurt seems to increase, as time goes on
Even though you held on to your undying faith so long
Oh, what a battle it is to hold fast with all you might!
A heart-wrenching struggle- a brutal, never-ending fight
Daily, we climb mountains, only hoping to reach the top
Stumbling over rocks, losing grip, and occasionally coming to a
complete stop
Confused, yet curious to see what is at the peak
Subsequently, we are out of breath and can hardly speak
I speak for myself, as I can only pray to hold on just a few
moments longer
I say, Lord, give me wisdom, heart, and please Oh please, make
me stronger

## Dreamer
On goals....

Dream a dream of a distant time or place
Dream to your heart's content at a forthright pace
Dream to the highest mountain – here, you can go
You can go anywhere in life and this you should know
No one can crush a will that is true to your heart –
Or dismantle a vision, tear your hope apart
You are the captain of your barge and the teller of your time
So use your moments wisely and caution every dime
This life is a fairy tale, just wishing to be unveiled
Your hands write your story and embellish your tale
Whosoever sets their mind, he shall accomplish great things
He controls his future and for him, the angels sing
Upon your greatest sleep, fantasy seems –
The drive that becomes reality and accomplishes your dreams

## <u>Dear Diary</u>
On mistakes....

Dear Diary,

I shall now speak my mind
For all of the years that I was legally blind
Towards the bold truths before me and the things I ignored,
When all my emotions were raw – emotions I now hoard.

How could I have been so naïve – such a child!
It seems it took forever for me to learn – a very long while.
Discovering what I know now was the hardest part,
Thinking all were to blame when it was I who broke my heart.
At this point, I admit that I could have dealt my cards better.
I acknowledge that now that I form the words to write this letter.

Life is surely a journey, used to teach the things you are
not soon to forget.
Consequently, it moves along at the speed of a pilot's jet.
Sometimes I wish I would have stopped to think -
About the things I missed, when I paused to blink.
I know there was so much I missed with my head in the clouds
And I believe a lot of which was evident and very loud.
Most mistakes I made repeatedly, as they should have gotten old,
Especially since I so often felt out alone in the cold.

I'm sure, in twenty years, I'll look back on the past.
While I realize sometimes I moved too slow and other times too
fast.

# Poems of Lessons

What a life it will have been, by then! There will be so much to
ponder on and quite a bit to sort through - a lot to make me feel
wonderful and more to make me blue. Either way the table turns,
I believe I will finally see,
That every single event that occurred will have made me, me.

Sincerely,
Brandy

## Be Real

You play the role of someone else and you are unaware
Of the things that you do, as you obviously do not care
While you smile in my face, you frown behind my back
From my front, you shake my hand, but from behind, you attack
I'm tired of your lies and I'm over all your games
You crushed so many hearts and put so many others to shame
You probably think it's okay, because you can't see others' tears
Because their self-esteem has been ruined enough, throughout
the years
It takes so much energy to put on your show
Why can't you just be truthful and be the one you really know?
There's a cloth of wool over your eyes if you can't see who you've
become
So don't even act like you don't speak badly of everyone
I just know that I am tired of being hurt; there is no more I will
take!
Because you say you're being yourself and you are just being
fake
No one believes you anymore; you are completely untrue
And you think you're fooling me, but the only one you're fooling
is you

## <u>Why Love a Lover...</u>
On discretion of feelings...

Why would you love someone who has no feelings for you?
How could you love another, whose heart, to you, isn't true?
It is hard to see how one would care for one with no care in
return
Or give emotions to a person - emotions they did not earn
It is painful to hold on to unrequited love's dream
As your heart never skips a beat and theirs always does, it seems
Love is certainly difficult and it loves no one, at all
This emotion is selfish and will never break your fall
There lies great chance that you will love someone that does not
love you back, because they are too busy doing the same
But it's hard, because when you love a non-lover, there is no *one*
to blame

## Stand Apart

On courage....

Who are you but one in the crowd -
Of those ashamed, afraid to be proud...
The world is a sea of followers with very few to lead,
Filled with drones, marching to a monotone creed
*He* resembles *she*, vice versa and the same
Similar in various ways, different only by names
Do you have no yearning to be exotic or unique?
Do not you consider *change* as one of your needs?
Glance beside yourself and see no change
In those on either side of you
How far apart do they range?
Listen close to all I say:
In a swarm of civilians, who is going to save the day?
Courage, intelligence, endurance, strength, heart
MLK, Queen Elizabeth, Napoleon Bonaparte
You have opportunity to be what most are not –
To be what he is afraid to be or what she *once* sought
Every single one that judged and hated and condemned
Will soon be those that will do *anything* to be your friend
To them, you will be the hero who escaped the doubt and the
fright
The one who broke away from the herd and dared to fight –
Dared to stand alone, with no one by your side
Dared to be scrutinized and envied, because you opened your
eyes
Some will always tear you down, beat and kick you on the
ground

## Poems of Lessons

Laugh when you cry, until the very day that you die,
But patiently wait, for God will reward your troubled heart
Because you stood atop the hill, unlocked your shackles, and...
*Dared* to stand apart

## <u>Wait</u>
On patience...

There is nothing but time in these days
Nothing but days in these years
For every ounce of patience we display
We receive kindly events that are dear
Virtues bring us the best
Because time unfolds on its own
Allow time and you will be blessed
A life worth living you will be shown
The best things are always prolonged
Every pearl needs time to form
Your fate will never be wrong
Destiny's treasures you will adore
We have nothing but moments to share
There is nothing but minutes to spare
Breathe only in the moment of one breath
Live life with no thoughts of death
Great jewels will flow with the wind
With the weeks, all hurt ends
All yearnings we have in this month
Will eventually transform into wants
Those wants will be needs we create
That we will acquire, if only we *wai*t

*Poems of Lessons*

## Redemption
On decisions...

Sitting in his cell, staring at his feet
Thinking of his destiny
He wipes away his tears-
Reflecting on past years
On years when this man was free
Goes back to the night; the knife in his hand
This crime he committed was grand
She lay on the floor - blood poured from her head-
For more than one breath, she treads
Simultaneously, their hearts beat, until hers fades away
This, too, is what he thought of, in the court room on the
sixteenth of May
Of only twenty-five, this man was ashamed at the verdict that the
jury gave
But five years later, as he sat on death row,
He strived and he strived to be brave

\*\*\*

Waking up in a space of an unknown bathroom stall
She rises to her feet but stumbles to a fall
At the peak hours of the morning, this girl wonders where she's
been
Looking in the mirror, she discovers a sin
With white powder-dust sprinkling from her nose
Trailing by her feet, splashed across her clothes
Once again she has given in to her addiction to this drug
Of all her distant feelings, she has been mugged

49

Somehow finding her strength, she makes her way to the street
Catches a ride; arriving on Delilah Avenue, she walks the
concrete
Reaching her house, she opens the door
She lets her torn and tattered shoes hit the carpet of the family
room floor
The two bold black eyes of her mother were staring dead in her
face
All she could do was make her way to the sofa at the slowest pace
A few words was all her mother had to say-
To make it what this girl would call her worst day
Before she knew it, she was being picked up and taken away by
an empty bus, as she said goodbye to the home she thought she
would never return
And in what seemed to be minutes, she was facing the
Rehabilitation Center of Albert Stern
She was whisked down the hall and into a vacant room, strapped
and confined to a hospital bed
The lights were turned off and no one was there; it was in this
dark room that she had to lay her head
*** 

Reclined on a bar stool on a Saturday night-
Taking down shots of Brandy, left and right
The man had a bad day at work, was dumped by his girlfriend,
and felt so blue
He also came to see that none of this bad luck, to him, was new
Depressed is the word that describes him the most
And stress is the thing that plays as its host
Every sip that he took drove him steeper to pain
He felt he had to take a drive or he would simply go insane

# Poems of Lessons

This man gathered up his strength, and made his way to the car
What happened next came to pass after he hadn't gone too far
He hadn't even gotten all the way down the street, when he felt
he was blind
Barely made two turns of the wheel, when he started losing his
mind
He didn't even realize he was on the freeway doing forty miles
per hour
Before he knew it he was screaming out with all of his power
Suddenly right off a bridge his car flew-
Into water that from the sky, appeared to be so blue
Maybe if he hadn't drank so much and noticed what could've
saved his life from ending in destruction:
The sign on the passing that read: Bridge under Construction

***

With a spray paint can in her hand, she thought she was
Michelangelo's double
But the only artwork this girl was used to was the art of getting
into trouble
With holes in her jeans, black nail polish and chains around her
neck, she tagged buildings for fun
But always hung with her gang, so when the authorities' flashing
lights beamed, she wasn't the only one
She maintained a "D" average in school, on the days that she
went
She gave only half the respect needed to her parents
This girl never did her chores or has never met her curfew
She always made it home, many hours past due
This was the only day she was walking the streets alone-
No friends to be with; on her hip was no cell phone

51

It was only a second that this girl looked down, at her feet
When a van pulled around and a pair of hands and her shirt did meet
She kicked and screamed in the arms of an unknown driver's help
In the backseat of an unknown van, with nowhere to run, all she could do was yelp
Her destination was unknown, but her feelings of fright were already overgrown
As she kicked and screamed, tears rolled down her cheeks and her life flashed before her eyes
But the place she arrived at next was of no surprise
She somehow knew this was the last place she would ever see -
Being carried away into the deserted warehouse, cold and dismal was she
This girl was thrown into a room and as the door was slammed, the little light from the outside was shadowed away
No more games with life were left for this girl to play
She curled up in a ball, tears dropping on her knees, clenched to her chest so tight
In a room clouded with the stench of evil and the black of night

*\*\*\**

It's almost human instinct to take advantage of life
Taking away the beauty in the world, in one simple strife
We have so many chances to start over in everything we do
Lessons presented as mistakes, received by us to be clues
What do all these people have in common as for decisions they made?
They ignored the virtues of life and covered them like a shade

The man sits in prison, because he murdered someone he thought he cared about
He chose an unbearable solution, over the course of screaming or to shout
He could've walked away from the marital problems with his wife -
Walked away, talked it out, and started a new life
The same solution goes for the girl and her addiction to cocaine
She could've asked for help or tried to say no, and good her life would remain
And as the good escaped from the man and his drink-
He could've consulted a psychiatrist, cleared his mind so straight he could think
Think- the one thing that the girl who was kidnapped should've done -
Made better in her life, made better for everyone
All four of these people had chance after chance to bring light into their lives
Instead of turning to gangs, drugs, drinking, and even knives
Now, sorrow is the word that describes them all
They may not turn the clock back, because they've taken a fall
They wish they could've said goodbye to the ones they love
As for the man of the drinking, before he went up above
They wish they could've asked for forgiveness of those that they hurt
As for the girl in the gang, because she was so curt
If only they had the opportunity or just the time
To go back and make it right, or better, sublime
See, all these people roaming the earth think they have eternity to live

*Poems of Lessons*

Not knowing that tomorrow's day could be the last breath you
give
It's somewhat like a bomb waiting to go off
Like a timer on an oven; now you scoff
But these words that I speak are so true, because the time on this
earth is limited for me and you
Always try to do right, when you get the chance
And if you fail and make a mistake, fold those hands
I hope and pray you will make better decisions than the ones in
these stories, as they haven't gotten the chance to receive or
mention...

Redemption

## In the Treasure Chest

There is a jewel in a box at the bottom of the ocean –
Hidden amongst the sea
In a flask, it sits like a pungent potion
Untouched, it's perfect; it rests so brilliantly
It's hunted for and longed for by the vast majority
Shall you feast your eyes on this great spectacle
It may rob you of your sight
Because some things are so remarkable
When you have them, it doesn't seem right
Stumbling across great treasures
Should be appreciated and enjoyed
These items can bring you pleasures
Of unknown exuberance and joy
A blessed fishermen anchors down and hooks on
To something of great weight
Upon the beauty of a great dawn
He may hoist up this enormous crate
Inside may lay a jewel, which he gazes at, for long
His grubby hands deceive him and it falls back into the pond
Tears reach his eyes, as he fumbles in the water – sheer
As the pond becomes an ocean and the jewel quickly disappears
The jewel will sink back to the sand
But he can get it back, he must
He thinks maybe he can't
Because the jewel he lost was trust
It floated back to its box, twenty leagues under the sea
To form into a diamond for the next voyager in need

## Tear Ducts
On **expressing** emotions...

Each of us is equipped with all we need
With every element of life that helps us to succeed
We have nothing on our body that serves no use
These same parts *can be* subject to abuse.
Still, we have hands to help us *feel* the way
Through this vast jungle that we encounter, every day
Our legs take us every place we wish to go
While our minds store every idea we need to know
We sense with our intuition when we are not aware
With ears we hear all we dare...
If we touch with our hands and we see with our eyes,
Why do some not take the time to cry?
Emotions serve a purpose and were given for a reason:
To be embraced within every moment, not just certain, particular
seasons.
If we do not feel what we feel
We become prisoners to God's gift to man
To the wounds that will never heal
While we hide behind our hands –
Hide from raw emotions and hurt, thereof
By even those things caused by the gift of love
Open up your heart to let the bad blood flow
Reveal what is within and let the pain show
Open up your mouth to scream out your insides
Unleash your soul through your eyes
Make yourself transparent, if only for a short while.
Experience the essence of it all, if only for a mile

# Poems of Lessons

Natural is being devastated when out of every ounce of luck
Which is what we miss when we dodge and duck
If we are not supposed to sob,
Why would God give us tear ducts?

## The Eleventh Hour
On departures....

I am upon my departure but my love will remain
It will scintillate boldly through all the tears and the pain
This will be a challenge and you will see that it will hurt
But it never has to be something brash or something curt
We have spent many moments in high spirits and smiles
As our bond has been strengthened and lasted all the while
True friends we have become and memories we have shared
Many times of fellowship, camaraderie, and care
We were bound to have to separate at one time or other –
To have to test our friendship for the sake of one another
No memories can be stolen from us and our time will never be
forgotten
In our minds they will be fresh – still active and trotting
If you are true to me, time away will only give us joy
Because your friendship was real – never treated as a toy
We will confide in one another just the same as we always have
Just as we have so far, as we've traveled down this path
Life may take us many places and scatter us about
But we are only physically divided, and all you have to do is
shout –
If you need me to be there, mentally, I surely will be
Because all that matters is that I love you, as you do me
If all we have is true, you will know I could never leave your side
Even with thousands of miles between us, I am only moments
shy -
Of hearing your daily issues and all your praise-worthy events
Or the situations with life that you tried to prevent

*Poems of Lessons*

Only a phone call away, I am still here when you cry
I am still in your life to help those same tears dry
We can still make it through the rain together and talk about our
fears
We should still never forget this time we've shared and all the
years
Yes, we will miss the personal contact, which we are used to
But a real bond can do without that, I do believe. Do you?
I still want to be your friend wherever I may go
Regardless of where I am, I will be forced to show –
How much you mean to me and all we have had
The distance, to me, will only be a tragic mishap-
One that will never ruin us or alter this bond in any way
Our times, I will keep in my heart every day
Make it through this journey with me and please hold on with
every ounce of your power-
Because your endurance will be wonderfully rewarded on the
very day I return,
We will have survived this suspension of time and my eleventh
hour...

# Short Stories

Enriching Tales of Shorter Length

"A man who does not respect his own life and that of others robs himself of his dignity as a human being"

Dalip Singh

## Compassion

There was a wonderful nineteenth century home with a beautiful garden of roses, lilacs, tulips, and herbs; a porch swing made of the finest wood and metal hinges; antique window shutters, and a fairly large backyard. The house was on Rose Street in a small, quiet town in Georgia and it was significant, because it always smelled of sweet treats and delectable foods that everyone enjoyed, especially because of the love and warmness that always came with it. This house was over fifty years old and it belonged to Ms. Edna May Ross, grandmother of 'Mac' Lynn Ross.

Normally, you would think of Mac as a boy's name, but in this case, Mac stands for Mackenzie Lynn and she is, indeed, a girl. Little Mackenzie was only five years old when she decided to be a tomboy; she never was one to worry about her hair or nails and she didn't like to take baths. In fact, she was often mistaken for a boy (just like the ones she loved to play with), because she loved to take her long braided ponytail and tuck it under her baseball cap. But, unfortunately for Mac, as soon as she turned around, you could see that she was actually a very pretty girl, because of her beautiful eyes and rosy cheeks and cute little nose that her grandmother just loved to pinch.

And that is exactly why Mac adored her grandmother so much; she accepted Mackenzie for her and not for the "swan" (a term her mother would use, so often) she *might* become. Mac always loved to hear anything her grandmother had to say, but she especially loved her majestic tales of adventure and the "olden days." She had a feeling that a few of the stories her grandmother told weren't true but at only ten years old, it didn't bother her enough to do any further investigation.

On another note, it was a hotter than usual summer day in this smaller town in Georgia that I told about. It was just about three-fifteen (fifteen minutes after Mac gets out of baseball practice), when the petite girl burst through the door of 315 Rose Street, kicking her old and dingy tennis shoes on the bright and freshly-vacuumed rug of her grandmother's house.

She tore her favorite red #33 baseball cap from her head, as she said in a loud, shrill voice, "Grandma Ross, I'm here! Grandma, where are you?"

Mac was certainly confused when she didn't see her grandmother rushing to her front door with a plate of freshly baked cookies and a pitcher of whole milk, but she figured Grandma Ross was busy doing something so she decided to close the door and make herself comfortable. Boom! Mackenzie closed the door, but the butterfingers she tended to have in baseball came into play and a picture crashed off the wall nearest the door.

Little Mackenzie was a brave soul, so she certainly wasn't going to get scared about what her grandmother would say, as she picked up the older photo with the now slightly cracked glass in the corner. She tilted her head in curiosity, peering at the photograph of a boy with ruffled hair and a queer-looking smile, who was sitting in a wheelchair with his feet straddled in a peculiar manner.

64

"No color," Mac whispered to herself, noticing the picture was black and white and gazing at it in her hand; she knew it was no one in her family and her curiosity began to grow.

Just as she said that, her grandmother's heavyset, sixty-two-year-old figure, wearing a longer homemade dress, suddenly appeared. Her long gray hair swayed behind her as her smaller eyeglasses were perched atop her slender nose on her warm and pudgy face.

Mac almost forgot about the picture (but still held it in her hand) as she dashed across the room to embrace her grandmother, hollering "Grandma Ross!"

Ms. Edna hugged her granddaughter dearly and smiled a dainty smile. "Hi, there, darlin'."

"Hi, Grandma. I was comin' into the house and I saw this here photo. Who is it?" Although Mac was happy to see her grandmother after a long day at practice, she was still awfully curious to find out who the mysterious boy in the photo was, so she bought the photo into her grandmother's view and grinned inquisitively.

Ms. Edna took only a glance at the photo, at first, but noticing who it was, she looked a little more interested and it soon brought a very grand smile to her face. "That, Mac, is someone special... Someone very special."

After grabbing the cookies from the kitchen, Mac found herself lying on the floor of her grandmother's parlor as her grandmother rocked in her favorite rocking chair. Mac stared at her grandmother with eyes of wonder, as her snack sat neatly beside her.

Grandma Ross contentedly held up the black and white picture of the odd-looking boy in the glazed pine oak frame, smiled and sighed briefly and then began: "This picture here takes me back a long ways. Let's see..." the older woman paused to think, "It's 1992 right now and this picture was taken way back when I was about your age in 1940... Yes, that's it 1940."

Grandma Ross continued the story as if she was engulfed in the atmosphere of it all and she was right back in the place in time that the picture described. "I remember it like it was yesterday..." She laid her head back and began to rock in her chair, as if she were embarking on a dream. "I was goin' to school at a real old school house and that was in the days when Georgia was practically nothin' but a bunch of woods. And I know we had to walk miles just to get to the general store and there was pretty much nothin' in our town, back in those days. But, I do remember school, if I don't remember anythang else. I had to get up EVERY mornin' and go to school to get my education as my momma would say. And back in those days, we didn't have school like ya'll have school now..."

"You didn't, Grandma?" Mac very seldom interrupted her grandmother's stories, but she quickly caught herself and continued her fascinated look of attention, after the instant flush of apple red cleared from her cheeks.

"No, darlin'. Pretty much all the students between the ages of five and nine were in a separate part of the school house while ten all the way to maybe seventeen or eighteen schooled in the same building. And there were only about one or two teachers dependin' on the day. So, it was a big class. I had a few friends in my class that I was really close with and they were - hmmm, let me see - Penny Rochester, Dawn White, and Sally Otis. Now, Penny, Dawn, Sally, and I were pretty much the popular girls amongst our age group and a lot of the boys had a crush on us, so we could just pick and choose which ones we wanted to play with or talk to. And, darlin', when I tell you there were some handsome boys in our grade, I ain't lyin'.

"In fact, there was a real nice lookin' boy by the name of Andrew Polite and he was sharp lookin'. He had sandy brown hair and a nice physique for his age and he was real smart and he could play just about any sport you put before 'em. Everyone knew he liked me, but the thang they didn't know was that I didn't like him...No, ma'am, I did not. And it was because he was too caught up on himself and I couldn't stand that. I liked boys that kept themselves up and stayed nice and clean but didn't mind gettin' down and dirty sometimes, if you know what I mean. The girls always got on me about it and they really thought I was crazy for not likin' 'em, but I had my heart set and I was sure I didn't want 'em. But, anyhow, one day, we had all come into school early, because our teachers said they were expectin' a new student from Iowa and they wanted to make sure everyone would be there to meet 'em. They wouldn't tell us much about him except for the fact that his name was Billy Rain and that he was ten years old.

"So we were clueless until we came in, that day. And I'll tell you somethin', Macky, I had no idea that that was gonna be the day that would change my life forever. So, that day we all got into our best clothes and showed up just at the time that our teacher instructed us. We crowded into the schoolhouse room and sat at our desks to wait for the boy. That had to be the longest wait I had ever experienced or maybe it could've been because I was so anxious to see the new student. But for whatever the reason was, we waited…..and waited….and waited.

"Until suddenly…" the older woman's eyes widened as she rocked forward in her chair, "we heard the door creak and in came a boy bein' rolled into the room by a woman, pushin' his wheelchair. He was pretty average lookin' except for that dog-on contraption. I didn't mind it; he looked just as normal as the rest of us, other than it, but the rest of my classmates had some different thoughts about it, as they all started laughin' louder than a banjo player at a jamboree. I couldn't BELIEVE that they would do such a thang, but I must say, Macky, I was different and a little more mature for my age; I could understand thangs like that, but I guess my classmates surely could not. They laughed for a while until you could see tears runnin' down the boy's face and that was when the teacher calmed everyone down.

"The poor boy was so upset, that they had to take him home and he couldn't even stay for his very first day at school and I, well, I was mad - stark ravin' mad - at what had happened. But, I was more so concerned about the boy. After that day at school, I ran right home and told my momma, your great grandmother Pearl - bless her heart - and she was just as upset about the issue as I was, so we both baked cookies for me to take to the boy's house, once we had called the school to find out where he was stayin'. Once we did that, I raced just as fast as my little legs could take me, right on over to his house that happened to be not too far from mine; of course, not too far, back then, was quite a while, but I made it.

"When I finally did get there, I didn't take too well to the house, but I went ahead and rang the doorbell, because the boy and his family had a screen door and you could see clean through the house; but I didn't wanna open it without permission. But just to my surprise, Billy Rain came rollin' right up to the door so fast it almost frightened me. He just said "yes" in more of an agitated way - so agitated that I was almost afraid to answer. But I somehow came to the conclusion that I would have to answer him sooner or later or my mother's and my cookies would go to waste.

"I said hello and told him who I was and I also managed to tell 'em that I had brought the cookies to apologize for what had happened to him at school. What's funny, though, Macky, is the fact that he had a straight and somewhat cold face the whole time that I spoke, but it somehow seemed that he was really interested in what I had to say. After my explanation, he looked at me for a second and then slowly opened the screen door to take the cookies. He closed the screen door and looked at me for a second, once again, then said 'Thank you for the cookies, Edna…and, and, and the apology; I hope I'll see you at school tomorrow'. After that he just turned around and rolled away right back into his house. Normally with any other person, I would've thought of the way he handled the situation as rude or impolite but there was somethin' about that boy that made me think differently."

Grandma Ross folded her hands in her lap and went on as Mackenzie stared in awe. "So I went home and told my mother about it and the next day at school, as I sat in my seat and waited for class to start and talked to my three best friends, I, indeed, did see him roll into the room in his wheelchair, just the way he did the day before, only this time I was really excited to see 'em. He didn't have to pick a seat, but we glanced at each other a lot once he was situated and I couldn't stop thinkin' about him when recess rolled around.

"I remember I was playin' hop-scotch with my friends, when I went to get a sip of water from the water fountain; I put my head down to get a drink, but then I looked up to see that Billy Rain was right there waitin' for me to look up at him and when I finally did, he asked me if we could talk. Me and Billy Rain talked for a long time, that day; we talked about what had happened the day before and just about everythang there was to know about each other.

"He turned out to be a very wonderful boy - one that I had described, opposed to the type of boy Andrew Polite was. He was very interesting and fun and just an all-around great person to be with and the good thing about that whole thang, Macky, was that he felt the same about me. We talked every day during recess and it got to the point where we were talkin' even after school. Now, my mother wasn't too fond of it, but she really couldn't help it when she figured out how great of a boy he was. My friends didn't take too well to me bein' friends with a 'cripple' as the school called 'em. But you know, Mac? I didn't really care. To this day, that boy was one of the most decent boys I have ever met

70

and at that point of my life, he meant a whole lot to me and everyone could tell.

"It wasn't long before I was considered the joke of my class, but it was worth it to witness the friendship of Billy Rain's and mine grow. It wasn't long before school was out for summer and it was hot enough for me and Billy to go to the lake that was closer to my house than it was his, but he didn't seem to mind it – not at all. So, we would meet up at that lake just about every day after chores and breakfast and I would swim most of the day, while Billy watched and loved it more than I did swimmin'. I used to beg him to get in with me the first few times we went, until he finally told me that he couldn't swim because of his legs; he told me he had never learned to swim or never had the chance to, but I had convinced myself that maybe if he watched me swim enough, he would learn to.

"But one day, it was just after lunch when I called Billy and we decided to go to the lake for a little while, so I threw on my favorite swimsuit and I met Billy there, just as we always had that summer. I dove straight into the water head first, just like any other time but, this time, it was different; when I started to come up, I could feel somethin' put a strain on my leg and I couldn't move." Mac gasped at that and you could clearly see the fright in her eyes. "I struggled and struggled to get out of the water, as I could hear Billy above water, cheerin' for my dive. Little did he know that while he was cheerin' with all his might, I was strugglin' for air below the surface."

Mackenzie's eyes got bigger and bigger as she listened to her grandmother go on.

71

"At that very moment, all I could think of was Billy's face and the fact that if I didn't get back to the surface in time, I would never see it again. I think it was that thought that fixed everythang, because all the sudden I could see Billy plungin' through the water so fast, as he headed for my feet and he used his strength to pull me out of the undercurrent that was about to carry me away. I couldn't think of anythang but gettin' free and when I suddenly did, I could feel a huge weight bein' lifted off me while I floated to the surface and took the deepest breath of my life.

"I swam to the side and hoisted myself out of the water, coughin' and goin' on, until I suddenly thought about Billy and the fact that he couldn't swim, but when I finally got the strength to even get up, I realized it was too late and Billy wasn't gonna come back up to the surface, that day. But it took a few weeks for me to realize that Billy saved me and pretty much killed himself that hot summer day in Georgia." Grandma Ross's eyes began to glaze over but the tears never fell. "All I could do was cry so hard my stomach crunched inside my body and delivered a pain worse than childbirth, as I let my hand fall on the seat of the wheelchair the poor boy drove...the only thing left of Billy Rain.

"That seat and this photo." Grandma Ross held up the photo of the deceased boy and she could see her granddaughter crying the heaviest tears she had ever seen. "Do you know what this story teaches you, Mac?" Ms. Edna sat calm and collected in her chair as she stopped in her rocking and asked the meaningful question.

"I'm not sure, Grandma," Mac said through her tears of concern.

"It teaches about compassion - the trait of being able to give others something you don't know whether or not you would give yourself, the feeling of unconditional love for someone that you would do something for them that you would never in a million years do for yourself. I never expected anythang like what happened when I befriended that boy all those years ago, but it took compassion out of me to be a good person and do somethin' for someone that I would want them to do for me. The reason I keep this picture is because just about everyone in my school thought of that boy as a queer, troubled, little boy, but I'll always remember him as not just a weirdo, not just a silent bein', and not just a "cripple"; instead, I'll remember Billy Rain as the fun-lovin', wonderful young man that saved my life that day in Georgia, and traded his for mine in the process."

Little Mackenzie lingered on the last words of the story, and - just like all the other times - was not the slightest bit disappointed in this particular story itself, as it just might have been the best story she had ever heard.

"To forgive is to set a prisoner free and discover that the prisoner was you."

Lewis B. Smedes

## Dear Diary
On forgiveness...

*May 12, 1988*

*Dear Diary,*

*Today is the day right before my 16th birthday and Momma decided to give me my present, a day early; it's a scarlet diary with a locket shaped like a heart and it came with a key. I think the reason Momma gave it to me was to cheer me up since Jerry couldn't be with us on my birthday. Ever since he passed away last week, Momma has been telling me that his passing was for the better and that everything would be all right, but every night I lay awake with tears rolling down my cheeks, I am veered to believe the opposite.*

*Another reason why I've failed to believe this is because ever since Jerry passed, Momma has been secretly crying almost non-stop every time she does the laundry and comes in contact with Jerry's old clothes; it's gotten so bad that she had to bundle them all up and put them in a secret place in the attic. Pa has chosen to show his sorrow by anger; lately I have found him starting arguments with Momma over the silliest things and when he starts to drink....let's just say he's not himself any longer. I hate having to wake up in the morning and I dread trying to go to sleep at night, because all I can do is think of my brother; I feel like my life has become nothing but a worthless wreck and lately, I've only been asking God why He didn't let me die right along with Jerry. I can't even look in the mirror without seeing his face and sometimes I make myself believe that if I dream about him enough, it might bring him back...but it never works. And as if things couldn't*

75

*get any worse, I have decided that last night was the worst night of my life; Momma and Pa got into an argument and it ended in a way I would have never imagined I would ever have to witness...Recently, many things have threatened to tear us apart as a family - Jerry's death being one of the most obvious - but I have a feeling that this just might be the hand that secured the lock on the casket after the death of our family, passing with the soul of Jerry.....*

*Sincerely,*
*Jennie*

*I signed: "Sincerely, Jennie" on the bottom of the page but I was born Jennifer Anne Dawson. Back then, I lived in the small town of Portland, Oregon in a small cottage more towards the countryside of Portland with my momma, Mary Dawson and my Pa, John Dawson.*

*Around the time that I wrote this diary entry, my family had just suffered the great loss of my brother, Jerry Keith; he had died from a sudden case of leukemia, after months of silently suffering from the disease. None of us knew he had it and in the beginning, the doc-tor just kept telling us that it was a fever and cough that would clear up, eventually. I think he didn't know what it was and was just wishfully thinking. Either way, it was the worst surprise of all of our lives when it turned out to be cancer. Momma and Pa and I had all stood by his bed side, where he spent the majority of his time, and helped him as much as we could during his time of need. But I was the one who cared for him the most. Momma was out running errands most of the time and Pa was out working at the lumber yard most days, so I assumed the responsibility of being his keeper - a labor of love that I cherish to this day. My brother was my idol, my best friend and we were closer than most identical twins; he was only a few minutes older than me,*

76

*but he was always there for me before he had the cancer and I felt it was my duty to do the same unto him, especially during the time that he needed me the most.*
*Jerry and I never let our relationship be endangered by anything, even when he was diagnosed.*

*Momma would sometimes have to come into his room late nights and make me go to bed after being in there most of the day and by that time, most of the night. I loved Jerry with most of my heart and much of my soul and I definitely showed that by taking care of him the way I did - changing his sheets every day, bringing him his breakfast, lunch, and dinner on time, feeding it to him, reading him his favorite stories from when we were kids, making him laugh with all his favorite jokes, telling him everything he might feel like he's missing (the news) from town, and even sneaking him for walks to the pond after dark, when Ma and Pa were asleep.*

*With all the time we spent together, you could never understand how I felt the day I walked into his room to give him breakfast, right when Momma had started her gardening and after Daddy had already taken the car to town. I had the biggest smile on my face, ready to give him his grits, toast, and orange juice (one of his favorite breakfasts) but that smile quickly faded away, when I saw Jerry lying in the bed looking too pale for words. I dropped the tray of food on the floor and as all the dishes crashed to the ground, I dashed over to my brother's side.*

*I quickly felt his forehead and felt for his pulse; there was none. After screaming and wailing for my mother and begging him to breathe...just breathe...just please breathe... I pretty much blacked out and the next thing I remember was standing around Jerry's coffin at his funeral, crying tear after tear alongside my momma and pa.*

# Short Stories

*Standing there with my parents and a few other close relatives of mine, all I could think of was all the times Jerry and I had together before he passed and all the times we wouldn't get to have now that he was gone. That day was the worst day of my life and now that I think of it, I really wish I could've had the diary Momma gave me, right then - right then, when I was standing in the vast field of forgotten souls, crying the hardest I had ever cried in my life, feeling I had lost my best friend, the person I almost loved more than anybody...Half of my soul and my person died that day and I think I lost all sense of hope for everything.. I stood there, frozen in time, staring at this box they had him caged up in, seeming to secretly die inside...like my only true friend, my brother...*

*During the next few days after Jerry's passing, I found it hard to be excited about my birthday, dealing with the circumstances, and I had a feeling my parents did, too. Every time Momma passed Jerry's room, I would watch her flee to another room just to collapse into a fit of sobbing; I knew she missed him more than anything. I knew Pop did, too, but since he was the man of the house, I guess you might've already figured the fact that he was working more than ever so he had no time to even try to grieve over Jerry the way he knew he wanted to. Pa worked at the local lumber yard and late nights were beginning to become closely affiliated with hearing him and Ma arguing over unwashed cups in the sink or dirty blinds in the living room. I was also used to catching Pa drinking on the cellar steps, after a while; it shocked me, at first, but unfortunately, I got used to it.*

*He never knew I was even there. The only reason I would catch him is because I would sometimes do the washing for my mother, after nine, when it was cool out, and I would come across the cellar, when it was time to hang the clothes to dry. I couldn't help but to peer around the corner and into the cellar* to see what Daddy was doing. Honestly, I thought my father would be able to drink at nights and be what they call "civilized" by day, but obviously, it wasn't the case. Daddy's personality changed, once he started drinking, and the sad thing is I don't think he could control it any longer.

...Which brings me to a couple days before I got the diary. I had just stepped off the school bus, parked in front of my house. I clutched my books a little tighter in my arms and began and began to shake my head as I could hear arguing coming from our house. It was around one o'clock and I knew Daddy was home for his lunch and was probably stressed out from work - maybe that was the cause of the argument.

From outside the house, all I could see were the outlines of my parents' bodies and their arms going up in the air and I could hear bits and pieces of the argument as I got closer to the house, while the rest was merely muffled speech. When I finally did get inside, Momma and Daddy were ranting and raving right in the middle of the dining room and my eyes widened, as I stared in frightened awe.

"What do you expect, John? All I do is work hard to keep this house together while you're away," Momma was sternly saying. I was trying to make my way to my room; my parents never really shouted at each other, and I didn't want to give myself the chance to hear them do so.

Unfortunately, Daddy needed a second person's opinion; I had no idea why he did what he did next, but my ankles had started to quake and my heartbeat picked up.

"Well, let's ask Jennie, here." My father was clearly insane at that very moment and only wanted to prove he was 'right,' just for the sake of doing it.

My mother was truly disgusted as she seriously beckoned him to stop, saying, "John, don't you do that to that girl." Then she turned to me. "Jennie, go to your room, honey."

"Yes, Momma," I said, my head down, but Daddy interrupted me.

"No, Jennie, tell your momma how it's lazy and absolutely disgusting to leave unwashed dishes in the sink."

By that time, Momma was as frustrated as ever. Her forehead was drenched in sweat and you could tell by the way she wiped her tangled hair out of her face that she was tired and ready for the argument to be over (sort of like a bad dream or a nightmare that you couldn't wake up from). "Jennie, please go to your room, honey." I could see she was very close to tears.

# Short Stories

I really felt her pain, as I hurriedly walked to my room, shaking and still frightened. As I did, I could hear my father starting up again, still hollering about the dishes. I could see Momma plunging unto the couch in distress, as I peeked through my cracked door.

"Look at me, Mary. What - now you don't want to listen? Fine, Mary! Fine! I'm going back to work." Then Daddy stormed out of the house, slamming the door and leaving Momma emotionally torn in two.

Sadly, that wasn't nearly as bad as you might think it was. Although Daddy used to never be one to treat my mother disrespectfully, at that point of their relationship, my father's drinking was tearing the two of them apart. I was just sad I had to be the one to pick up the pieces.

After I was sure Daddy was gone, I slowly cracked my door, folded my arms as if I were embarrassed or timid, and made my way into the living room. There sat my mother on the couch, with her head hung low in her hands, her hair draped over her face, but not enough to cover the tears she was crying. It hurt me to see this, as I began to walk toward her, not completely sure if I should or if Momma wanted me to. I was completely confused and all I knew was I wanted to comfort her.

**81**

*Short Stories*


I stepped toward her and just as I extended my hand, trembling uncontrollably, she sensed my presence and without looking up, barely mumbled, "Please, Jennie. Not now."


It almost brought me to tears the way Momma was so upset over the event or more so embarrassed that she didn't even want my hugs or comforting words. To this day, I don't really know what I would've said had she let me, but I do know she didn't. I just turned around and walked back to my room to do my homework trying to hold back my own tears in the process.


Later that night, the dinner table was as quiet as ever. The only noises heard were the clinking and clanking of the silverware and plates and the wind blowing in the window to cool the house. As there was hardly nothing to be said, I sort of wished Jerry was there to make everything better; his personality was always so warm and welcoming and there was always something about him that made everything bad or depressing seem like something to laugh about or easy to forget. I found myself missing his smile and his corky jokes and then I lost my appetite.


Momma interrupted my thoughts when she clearly only asked out of politeness, "How was school, honey?"

I choked out the words in a hesitant state, trying to conserve the little calmness I had left. "It was great, Momma. I'm doing really well in Language Arts and Biology, but Math isn't coming so easy." I was trying so hard to keep from getting up and leaving the dinner table. The only reason I didn't want to leave was because I didn't want Momma to think I wasn't enjoying her cooking. And lately, I had become afraid to leave my parents alone together, fearing that I was to come back to see one of them lying on the floor murdered while the other stood over the body, holding a bloody knife and evilly grinning about the crime they had just committed.

But it slightly amused me that through her own personal problems, Momma could find a way to remain the wonderful mother she was. "I'll look into getting you a tutor; Ms. Ralsin isn't busy on weekends, or better yet, I might be able to help you myself. I'm not too shabby in math." Momma seemed to be very supportive of me, despite her sadness deep inside; although, it seemed - as I said - that she was only trying to fulfill her duties as a mother, or better yet, ignore my father, who had decided to scarf down his meal as soon as possible and leave the table.

I didn't really want to include him in the conversation, but I was stuck between not talking to him and upsetting him even more than he already was or including him and most likely upsetting myself when I didn't get the response I wanted. "How...how was your day, Daddy?" I asked hesitantly, thinking I shouldn't have had to feel nervous at all. After all, he was my own father.

"*Fine, darlin'.*" *He just wiped his mouth, grabbed his plate as he headed to the kitchen only to plop it down in the sink, and left the dining room. I flinched when the dish crashed.*

*My mother just continued to eat her meal, but when he passed her, it was as if his presence caused her spirit to flutter. I hate to say it, but my father was beginning to have the very same effect on me. Sadly enough, I thought of this later that night, when I glared at Daddy, drinking on the cellar steps again. Something inside caused me to grow livid and disgustingly disappointed in my father - the man who was supposed to provide for us when we were in need of things, protect us from those that wished to hurt us, and love us unconditionally for as long as his heart would allow him to.*

*I could never know the troubles of someone else to their fullest extent, but whatever you might have been through, whether it's heartache or some other painful experience, such experiences cause you to have the ability to understand what I felt as I watched my father drink the alcohol and his life slowly but surely began to be devoured by hateful thoughts and actions - thoughts which he was destined to make his reality. It was like battling with myself. I was starting to hate him, but trying to love him, realizing the fact that it was just grief and damage to his soul.*

# Short Stories

We all had our own specific way of grieving over my beloved brother and I was reminded of this as I made my way into the house. As I passed Jerry's room I could see through the cracked door that Momma was clutching her stomach in her hand and bending over my brother's pillow, crying so hard her face was apple red. This was the sight that sickened me the most, witnessing the sweetest woman in the world being punished so, in so many different ways; it was all coming at her too fast to cope with and causing her to feel overwhelmed with feelings she had never had before or any idea how to control. I figured that even if I went in the room and tried to comfort her, it would end just as disastrously as it had earlier that day and I couldn't bear that - not one more time, so I decided to make my way to my room instead, saving myself the time and disappointment in the process.

I showered briefly after getting to my room and when I got back, I realized it was as if the whole day was finally beginning to dawn on me as I carefully placed my dirty clothes into my hamper and turned off my light. Everything was so upsetting and...overwhelming. As I pretended not to notice, during the day, it reminded me how terribly it would affect me when I laid my head to my pillow at night.

I couldn't help but cry, letting all the memories of the day and the week before flood back to me. Jerry...Jerry...my sweet brother - I wondered why he had to go away and wished he didn't. Everything was terrible! All the time, I felt my mother, father, and I were drowning in a pool of water, *gasping for air and only Jerry could save us. It was a pool of water just like the one I was creating on my pillow. I was wishing my mother would let me comfort her and I could've kissed her goodnight, something I hadn't been able to do in days because I didn't have the guts. It was such a heart-wrenching and awful situation. I had never in my life felt so hopeless, broken and confused. I felt like God was punishing us for things we had no control over. "Why didn't I pay closer attention to him?" I asked myself that night, thinking of Jerry and our walks to the pond; but I knew it was silly and that I was just upset. We all were and that was the worst part of it all; I just turned over and cried myself to sleep...*

Sadly, the situation between my parents, after my day at school, wasn't the situation I was referring to in my diary entry; little did I know, it was only the tip of the iceberg.

The next morning, after a long cry the night before and a stomachache, I had breakfast with my mother (my father was gone again), and I was happy that we finally had a chance to talk, even if it would only be a few words. Sitting at the table with my momma, I slowly drank my orange juice, staring dead at her reflection on my plate, wondering what to say, but that quickly faded when I remembered she was still the same person, just a little damaged.

"How'd you sleep last night, Momma?" I asked, barely looking at her but very interested.

In the strangest way, she looked a little better, as she ate her toast and began to answer my question, "As well as I could, darlin'." She paused and sighed as if she wanted to say more - the truth, perhaps. I could understand why she wouldn't want to tell me; Momma always tried to keep up with her emotions and be secret about them if they seemed the least bit overbearing, in order to keep calmness in the house. She sighed and began again, "I'm going to run to the bank today to set up a new account and do some shopping in town. I won't be back until a little later - maybe after you're out of school. I'll need you to start on dinner when your homework is done. Would that be alright, Jennie?" My momma looked at me on the last part, as if it truly mattered to her and the sincerity in her eyes made it that much harder to resist. I wondered why she needed a new account at the bank.

"Sure, Momma. I'll make your favorite for dinner," I answered, still thinking of the bank and the needy look in her eyes.

"Thank you, honey. You're a real help." I might have actually seen a smile on my mother's face as she continued to eat her breakfast; it made me so happy to have even said a few words with her after all that had been going on. I smiled back and continued eating.

After breakfast, I went to school, which let out early, and I came home to do my homework and cook dinner like Momma asked. I was making her favorite as I said: chicken-fried steak, mashed potatoes, and creamed corn. It was pretty nice to have the house to myself to collect my thoughts and be free to breathe without feeling afraid or oppressed by the overbearing tension that seemed to flow throughout the house, almost incessantly. But the hours seemed to fly by and soon the food was done and I was surprised Momma wasn't home yet; just when that thought entered my mind, my father came in the door. My heart jumped as soon as his boots hit the wood floor beside the doormat. I was studying some history homework in a chair in the kitchen, while trying to find ways to keep all the food warm without running up the utility bill, when I noticed my father was on the verge of a tantrum.

He slammed the door behind him and flung his coat on the coat rack, barely making it onto one of the hooks. His face was flaming red as he glared at the floor and scratched his ruffled brown head of hair before wiping the sweat off his forehead.

I looked like a deer caught in the headlights of a pick-up as I stared at him, cautious as to what he was going to do next; it seemed as if he were searching for words through his anger, but I figured I could calm him down a bit by saying hello. "Hi, Daddy." The words barely crept out of my mouth in a slight whisper, as I slowly closed my book; my attention wasn't on it anyways.

# Short Stories

"Ya Momma never came home, huh, Jennie?" he asked, but he seemed like he wanted to blow our house down right before me. For some reason, I was so afraid that he was going to hurt me, but I remained calm; I wanted to find out what exactly he was so upset about.

"No, Daddy. She didn't." I was afraid to admit, but I only wanted God and myself to know about Momma and the bank. For some reason, that seemed to be something I needed to hide.

He grabbed his hair as if he were going to pull it out while he paced in the same two steps like a mad-man. "God dern it! That woman is gonna rack my nerves! Wait 'till she gets home!" By now, he howled like a lion, livid and filled to capacity with rage.

I wanted to whimper "Daddy, please don't be so mad," but I couldn't bring my fragile mouth to do so; all I wanted to do was crawl under the table and hide. I knew, at my age, it wasn't the most mature decision, but my father had never gotten so upset when my mother wasn't home and at that point, I wasn't quite sure what Daddy was capable of. These thoughts trailed back in forth through my mind - like Mrs. Davidson's children running through the house when I used to babysit - just as I could feel my hand slowly creeping for the knife drawer nearest me. I wasn't sure if I meant to do it, but when I reached a certain age and thought back on it, I believe

89

*it was just out of pure instinct to protect myself. But, to my surprise, my father was far too upset with my mother to fool around with me and had decided to storm off to his room.*

*When he had finally left, my hand fell to my side and my heartbeat lowered. I let out a deep sigh of relief. I tried not to be so worried about my own safety, still thinking of my mother. I didn't know what to think of her - I mean, she had gone to the bank, after talking to me about an account, that morning, out of the blue and only God knew where she had really been all day after or before that. But, in my heart, I felt I wanted to call her, to warn her of my father's anger before she got home, but there were no numbers for me to call since I didn't know where she was or, for that matter, where she had been. All I could do was try to take a deep breath and pray to God that by the time Momma got home, Daddy would have cooled down. But, at that time, I was scared out of my wits and I didn't know if I could shake it.*

*A little later, after calming myself down and somehow bringing myself to read a book, I was perched on my bed in my room. Just when I was getting relaxed and figured everything had finally blown over with Daddy, (the house had been extremely quiet since his little interrogation), my head popped up from my the romance novel and my heart rate raised again, when I heard keys entering the front door of our house. I jumped out of bed, quickly wondering where Daddy was and if I could get to Momma before he could. A million questions began to scatter in my mind, as I clenched at my hair,* prepared to pull it out from mixed feelings of stress, fright, and almost...anger, because of the fact that I didn't know what to do and I only had a few seconds to decide. I could hear the key turning in the door and my fright increased, as more and more questions poured into my mind: Where was Daddy? Do I have enough time to get to Momma before he does? Where has she been all this time? Why didn't she call and tell me so I could've been prepared to cover for her? What would Daddy do to her if I didn't get into the living room in time? Would Daddy shout at her like the day before? What should I do?

I was more frantic than ever when I heard the door being completely unlocked and opened. All I could bring my feet to do was dash to my door and open it to go out, while my mind felt almost frozen solid. But when I heard Momma come in, all I could see in front of me, as my face seemed to freeze over, was my father walking right by my door and into the living room. I had failed; my father would make it into the living room before me, and no matter how worried about her I was or how much I had missed her that day and wanted to say hi and give her a big hug, I couldn't. I almost felt tears coming to my eyes, that very moment, as I gripped the door handle tighter and tighter, opening it more, while I thought about the fact that Daddy hadn't even seen me when he walked by. All I could do was listen and I didn't think I would like what I was about to hear.

I could see my father neatly and calmly lean up against the edge of the wall in the dining room as my mother's body froze in its place; she wasn't prepared to hear what he had to say. "So, you care to tell me where you've been all day, Mary?"

My mother already looked annoyed and tired as she threw her hands to her sides and let out a deep sigh. "John, what do you want from me? I'm tired, so please ask exactly what you want or I'm going to lie down." I was somewhat proud of my mother for being so bold, but I wasn't sure if this was the best time to display the act of bravado.

"No, Mary. Tell me where you've been all day. I have the right to know where my own wife is after a day of hard work and sweat!" Daddy's anger seemed to begin to be escalating when he took a few steps toward Momma, raising his back from the wall and looking her clean in the eye.

"John, I....I just went to run errands! Why can't you just leave me alone?" Momma replied. She looked like she wanted to collapse on the floor from exhaustion or stress as she tried to walk past my daddy.

"Now you just wait one minute there, Mary Jane Dawson." My father took my mother's arm and backed her up against the wall by the door. At this point I was afraid I was a little more frightened than my mother, seeing the fright begin to arouse in her eyes, or maybe she was more surprised than *anything.* "Now, for the past couple of weeks, I've been putting up with your crap - anywhere from dirty dishes to sloppy living rooms and everything else. Now, what makes you think you have the slightest right to talk to me like that?"

My mother was almost whimpering by now, as one single tear fell out of her eye and she stumbled to say what she had to say, wiping it away, "John, what are you doing? Jennie is..."

But my mother didn't get to finish what she was saying since my father decided to interrupt her, now shouting, "So, it's Jennie you wanna talk about, huh? Well, you wanna talk about how she's been your little slave worker for the day, huh! Huh, Mary!" My father was completely out of his mind, causing a tear to roll down my own cheek, which I quickly wiped away. My face was pressed into the crack of the door; I was trying not to miss a thing. I couldn't stand to look but I couldn't turn away.

"John, what are you talking about?" My mother didn't even raise her voice. I believe she was more scared than anything, even though my father had loosened up his grip on her arm.

"Don't give me that, Mary! Who do you think made this food in the kitchen, huh?" Daddy made his way to the kitchen and grabbed a pot. My mother yelled to stop him but he flung it onto the ground and after it, went another one. "No, Mary, you don't deserve to eat!" He threw the rest of the pots to the ground as my mother covered her ears and he marched toward her, every step driving me deeper and deeper into my self-created pit of panic. "And you think I don't know where you were all day, Mary! I know you were at that bank; word in town spreads faster than you think! What - did you think you could get away with it? Huh? You tryna leave me, Mary, huh?" My father grabbed my mother and shook her and then pushed her back, still livid with anger. I couldn't imagine her saying anything and she didn't. She just stood there crying, not sure whether or not she wanted to say something.

"Oh, now you don't wanna talk! Well, I guess you don't wanna talk about the dirty dishes, either then, Mary!" My father stormed back to the kitchen, and began to take stacks of plates and throw them onto the floor, following up with our bowls. My mother hollered how that was our good china and how expensive it was. My father continued on and said, "We don't need it; they never get washed! We don't need bowls, plates, spoons, saucers!" Every crash of each of those dishes ending up on the floor made my heart shrink more and more and my body stiffen in its place. I could barely breathe and I couldn't believe what I was seeing. I tried to move but my feet stayed in their place. I wanted to believe I was dead and wasn't in the house to witness what I was seeing or that I was having a terrible nightmare and I would soon wake up to see that it would all be over, but it wasn't and it just got worse.

94

# Short Stories

Through tears of fiery exasperation and maybe a little terror, my mother clenched her teeth and almost shouted, "John, stop it! Just stop it!" I couldn't believe she had done it. I don't know where she had gotten the energy or the strength to stand up to him, but she did, even if it didn't have the greatest outcome.

My father took a second to let what she had just said absorb and his face was calm and still and tranquil-looking, but you could tell that his insides were heating up like boiling water for tea. I could only imagine what he was going to do next. He took a few quick steps towards my mother and shouted in one simple sentence, "Stop, you say! You don't tell me what to do, woman!" And then....that very moment, my father did something I would've never expected in a million years, or maybe did expect but chose to ignore as a possibility - something that made my heart stop in its tracks and my spirit freeze, while cold tears of pain and sudden agony rolled rapidly down my, now, limp and barren cheeks. My father struck my mother across her face so hard and so fast it instantly brought tears to her eyes and a bellow from her mouth that I will never forget. I turned away in shock.

The room was calm and still and quiet for a moment while my mother held her face and tried to collect her dignity. Her purse and things had fallen to the floor from the force of the blow. My father looked like he liked the way hitting my mother made him feel and I guess he wanted to feel that feeling again, because he did it again and again and again

**95**

and again and again until my mother couldn't take anymore and was begging for him to stop, all the while she was holding his arms to shield herself from the burning sensation lingering on her face.

I just couldn't stand another minute of it. I slowly closed my door and collapsed to the floor, crying so hard I thought I was going to have an ulcer or a seizure. The thought of my father putting his hands on my mother sickened me and created a hate inside of me that I couldn't even fully realize because I was overwhelmed with tears that were now sinking into my carpet and creating a puddle. I felt like a coward for not helping her; I felt stupid for telling Daddy about Momma being gone all day (although he already knew); I felt like I wanted Jerry there to help me; I felt like God didn't love us and that's why He wouldn't help us; I felt like everything was going terribly and all I wanted was HELP! For the next hour and a half I wasn't surprised to hear more hitting and screaming and kicking and shouting and plates breaking and walls being hit by things and glasses breaking on the floor and things like "You're worthless!" and "You're stupid" and "I hate you" streaming like a screech of a demon streaming from the living room. It seemed like forever until it was all over and all I heard was the loudest, most disturbing crash of the front door slamming and my legs wanted to get up and go see what was going on, but it was as if my body wouldn't let me. But I somehow gathered my strength and slowly got up, cracking my door before I was even standing all the way up and letting my trembling hand help me the rest of the way.

My whole body was aching from crying so much and I could hardly bring myself to walk, when slowly....slowly...slowly, I crept out of my room and into the hallway, the slowest I had ever walked, with no thoughts in my mind, bereft of my feelings, but still desperately wanting to know everything thing that happened and more importantly, the condition of my mother. The scene I saw standing at the opening to the living room was indescribable, yet told me everything I needed to know in just one glance.

The cold of the room whisked about my body like the air of a dungeon and I felt my toes curl, as a heap of broken pottery seemed to suddenly appear beneath my feet. Apparently the windows were open and it seemed like a tornado had come right through our house, judging by the shattered glass, broken dishes, and food that I had made, all over the floor. Most of the pictures that were on the wall were either hanging half-way off or crashed and broken on the floor; our pottery and vases were scattered in different corners throughout the room, the furniture was moved out of place along with the dining room table and everything else was either broken or lucky not to have been touched. I had never seen a scene so horrific, especially not in my own home - the one place I felt safe and could relax without worrying about things happening like what had happened that day. But that was no more.

All in all, the house looked like a massacre had just occurred and there was no one to witness it; the damage had been done and the culprit had escaped, leaving only one wounded victim behind. My mother was curled up in a ball, facing the couch. That was the very worst moment of my life - seeing my mother in the fetal position, her legs so weak and frayed under her body - limp as if she had had her lungs snatched from out of her, sobbing her beautiful eyes out. I felt every ounce of her pain; she had never been beaten before in her life.

Tears quickly streamed down my pale cheeks and I didn't care how proud my mother had been or what she had been through or how much she might not have wanted me to. I went to my mother's side and comforted her. Through my own tears, I rolled her over to reveal her close-to-bloody cheeks, swollen, inflamed, and bruised, just the same as her ribs and stomach that I could only see because her shirt was folded up over her upper torso. I looked away for a moment in shock, as fresh tears fell from my eyes. She laid there like a corpse left to rot and I almost vomited at the thought of what had been done to her.

It was a horrifying scene, as I stumbled over my words, trying to comfort her until it finally just came out, "Momma....oh, Momma, please please talk to me, Momma....tell me...come on, Momma, get up....please, Momma." All I could do was lift her up, so that her back was leaning against the couch, as I, myself, felt limp. I was whimpering and choking over my words as tears cascaded to the floor and I reached out for her.

But I was totally surprised, when my mother nearly leapt into my arms and just clung to me. It instantly broke my heart all over again and she grasped me so tightly for so long, until she finally found the strength to cry out "Baby, darling, Oh, Jennie...Oh Jennie." She just repeated my name over and over again. I could feel her fears falling unto my back and I could barely hold her up because she was slipping out of my arms from her weakness. Still, I was just glad to have her in her arms. If only for a moment, I felt like I was the mother, cradling my child and she didn't want to let go. We stayed that way for a long time as we cried together, tears flowing so easily, because they were well-deserved and God knew it was our time...our time...our so deserved time to be together and cry together after our hurt and our pain. The dishes were broken and the pictures were smashed and my mother was beaten and Jerry was dead and the furniture was out of place and my father was gone and for some strange but beautiful reason, we both realized there was no more hurt to feel, no more pain to experience and it was all...just...over...

That, by far, was the worst night of my life; if I wasn't broken already, I certainly was, by then. I didn't know how to feel or what to feel or what to think or what to do, if I should do anything at all. While it was happening, it was as if I was dazed or sleeping and couldn't wake up, but as soon as it was over, I had woken up immediately and I was free. I couldn't help but to feel like a coward for not helping my mother, for not running to her side and defending her against my father. But then an image of his enraged and crazed eyes appeared in my mind and scared me away from the thoughts. I knew there was nothing I could have really done, but I still felt like I should have done something...anything.

After hugging for what seemed to be hours, I managed to get my mother to my bed. I didn't want to take her to her room because I had no idea if my father was coming home and I really didn't care. She hobbled along, her whole body aching, and I gently laid her on the pillow in my bed and slowly and softly placed the covers atop her. She never spoke, as she gazed up at me from under the covers looking like a small and fragile toddler, who had just experienced hell itself, but I could tell she was thankful for having me there.

Every time she blinked, it was as if she were drifting more and more off to sleep and I couldn't wait for her to do so; she deserved it and honestly, the pain in her eyes was killing me and making me want to cry again. I just wanted her to rest and try to forget everything - as if she could - and as soon as she did, I crept into the bed beside her, carefully putting the covers over the two of us as I put my arms around her and tried to fall asleep myself. We made it through until nightfall and it was all over

December 10, 1998

Dear Diary,

# Short Stories

Boy, do I have a story to tell! Out of pure excitement and joy, I'll shorten it and just come out and tell you that Mark proposed to me last night. Oh, it was like a dream! We were sitting under the dimly lit lights of our favorite Italian café, downtown, when he proposed to me, right then and there. What a gift for our five year anniversary! When he first showed me the ring, I was so ecstatic and not only could I not believe that he was asking me to marry him, I just couldn't bring myself to believe that we had been together for five years and that it has been ten years since I was such a young girl, living with my mother and father in Portland.

As he neatly slid the ring unto my finger and tears slid down my cheeks, it quickly reminded me how far I had come since then - from the times shared in the little cottage with my parents when Jerry was alive, to the rough times we experienced when he passed away, and especially from the last time I saw my father, ten years before, after he had beaten my mother almost unconscious. Sitting in that little Italian café with my fiancée in downtown New York City, I realized that it had been ten years since that horrible event had occurred and since I had first gotten this diary. I was promptly reminded that I was twenty-six years old; I had graduated from a prestigious college of photography in upstate New York; I own my own art gallery for my work and other artists; and I have survived all that has happened in my younger years.

I could not believe that my mother and I had made it through everything that happened to us, because even after the night that she was betrayed by her husband in the worst way possible, we still had to live with the lingering hurt and pain of it all. After that night, we were lucky to have not seen my father for a few days, which was just enough time for me to pack up all of our belongings (while my mother recovered) so that we could go away - anywhere, anyplace - just to get away from the place and time we were in.

It seemed like just yesterday when we had left Portland, running away like two little orphans to my aunt's house (the only family we had left on my mother's side) in Rochester, New York. Almost immediately, my mother had fought against her emotions to enroll me in a local high school and began working four jobs to save to put me through college. It brought me to tears some nights to know the struggle she went through just to keep me safe and educated and how much she went out of her way to be there for me and prove that she loved me more than anything in the world, now that we had no one else.

I couldn't even fathom, sitting in that café with my hand in the hand of my husband-to-be, that I, Jennifer Anne Dawson, was finally starting to be free from her past, free from the hurt and the pain...and was getting married.

With love,

Jenny

## Short Stories

Truly, it was remarkable that I had kept that diary all that time, but what was even more remarkable was all that had happened to me from the time I described in the memorable diary entry ten years before and the one presented above. The night I had to put my mother to sleep lingered in my mind, as I packed all of our clothes and things and even when we were on the bus to Rochester that same week. It lingered in my thoughts every day in high school, until the time I graduated and all the way up until the day I moved away from the apartment I had shared with my mother (after moving out of my aunt's house only a year before) to start college in the fall.

As I held my mother in my arms, thinking of all that she had done for me to get me to that point, I embraced her tightly and thanked her for everything she had put herself through for my own well-being, letting her know that I would be eternally grateful. I thought of that every day I was attending the school of photography in Albany and even more when I decided to move to NYC to pursuit my career in the same field. I wrote to my mother constantly, keeping her informed from the time I got my big break taking pictures for the *New York Times* all the way until the time I launched the grand opening of my very own gallery of photographs with some of my most highly-praised work. I would be a complete liar to say that I never thought of my father (the times we had before Jerry passed away) and how he never tried to find us or apologize to my mother for all he had done, but I could only give credit to my mother for my success, because in the end, she was the one that was always there.

Speaking of my photography career, shortly after I wrote the diary entry above, I had decided to take a day to enjoy the scenery of Central Park. Mark was planning to meet me afterwards for a cup of hot cocoa, so I decided to use the little time I had to snap a few shots of the breath-taking winter scenery that would be long gone sooner than I knew.

There it was, perched atop a burly maple tree - a squirrel stealing a tiny acorn from its resting place in the frosty New York afternoon. Somewhere in the middle of raising my camera lens to the sight, after wiping my red and frosted nose, I felt a tap on my shoulder. It might have made me jump a little because I was so focused on the photograph I was a few desperate moments away from taking, but not as much as the voice that followed - a voice that made me tremble at the start of it, a voice I hadn't heard in years, a voice that froze me in my tracks worse than the thirty-five degree weather of that day...

# Short Stories

December 12, 1998

Dear Diary,

I don't....I don't even know how to begin this entry. I don't even know where to start......All these emotions are going through me right now, but it's best to just........just come out with it.......Yesterday when I was taking shots for the gallery, at the park, I saw my father. I can't even begin to describe how I felt, how....anything...I couldn't believe it. I thought he was a ghost. I could've sworn my heart stopped beating, as I looked into his face. He literally came out of nowhere and right away, every emotion, every moment, every memory, everything just came flooding back. The tears I instantly cried seemed to freeze in the wind, when I looked him square in the eye for the first time in ten years........my father......after years of wondering and hurting and not knowing......my father.

I didn't make it to have cocoa with Mark yesterday, because.....it's a long story....But, I guess that's what a diary is for, right? .....I don't know. I panicked when I turned around and looked into his face. I didn't know what to say, what to do...anything, so I just ran. I turned right around and I walked away. All I could remember was the day he beat my mother and how he never called. My tears were falling to the ground just as fast as my shoes seemed to pound into the snow. I didn't know what was going on around me, but I could hear him following me, calling my name, telling me to stop, but I *couldn't....I couldn't face him...not after all he had done, not after how much he had hurt me.....not after all those years....But then I had no choice, because he caught up to me....and he grabbed me and held me, as I just collapsed into his arms and sobbed and I hit and scratched at him and I told him that I hated him and asked why he had left and why wasn't he there for me and why didn't he come for me. I screamed at him and slapped him ....but I still didn't let go ....and then I stopped and I just held him.*

*We seemed to stay that way for hours, as I could feel his tears fall unto my head....I realized I couldn't let go, because I didn't want to ....for some reason, half of me instantly forgave him. I don't know if it was because it had been so long or because I didn't want the vengeance or the hate or any horrible feelings I had in my heart anymore, or if I was just caught off guard or if I was falling for the fact that he must have went through a lot of trouble to find me or if I couldn't stop thinking about the father he was before Jerry died but either way it goes, I just let go of it all. I just let go.*

*Jenny*

*That diary entry came the day after what it actually described; the shock of everything that happened the day of prolonged it for just that long. Just as I said above, I had no idea how I was supposed to feel, what I was supposed to think, what I was supposed to do....when my father approached me that day in the park, it was as if every ounce of pain and hurt I once felt was fresh in my heart again and I really could not believe my eyes. As I said above, before I knew it, I was running away from him. After looking into the familiar face that had seemed to age more than the ten years I had not seen him, I was charging in the opposite direction to escape everything I remembered, everything that hurt, every memory that had haunted me for the past ten years. I ran as fast as I very well could, as tears poured down my face and I seemed to feel every ache and pain my mother felt when she was beaten and every dreary day Jerry experienced as he waited to die. But before I knew it, I felt two big strong arms surrounding me and a voice, begging me to stop, begging for my forgiveness and to see me, apologizing for everything that happened. It seemed as if I had blacked out, because the next thing I remembered was drying my swollen and red eyes, as I sat in the far corner of a coffee house nearby...with my father.*

*He stared at me from across the table as if I had been the only item to consume his thoughts all those years - not knowing what to say and looking just as frightened as a child, like if he were to touch me or even whisper to me, I would fall apart or melt before him.... "Jennifer, I don't know where to begin. I...."*

"What is there to say, John?" I peered at him with sudden uncontrollable anger in my eyes and in my heart that could not be put to rest, no matter how hard I seemed to try. "You beat my mother to a pulp for something that was not her fault. You left me, after my brother passed away and you left all the responsibility on my mother, like a coward! What a fool! You abandoned my mother...you abandoned me!" I was almost shouting through my even fresher tears, before he interrupted.

"Now, that's enough!" His tone was sharp and attentive and my eyes began to widen as I could only imagine what he could possibly have to say. "Yes, I was a coward; yes, I was fool, Jenny! You don't think I know that? After ten years, you don't think I know that I was stupid and downright wrong for what I've done? You don't think I've missed you terribly and that I..."

"So why wait so long! Why wait ten damn years, Pa! Why couldn't you be a man and come back when I needed ya - come back when it counted!" Right then, I just broke out in tears and sobbed. People began to look over at us and wonder what was the matter, so I decided to leave. "I can't do this." I grabbed my things as I headed for the door and my father called after me. I was running yet again and that time, I was determined not to let him stop me.

He charged out in the cold and I had already begun to fast walk down the block. "Jennifer Anne Dawson, I never stopped loving you! I was coward! I was a fool, but I realized....it may have taken me long...a damn long time, but I've realized what I've done and I'm sorry." Those words made me stop in my tracks in that cold New York air. I could hear a crack in his voice as he began to cry and some part of me also knew that he meant it. "I should've stayed! I should have never laid a finger on your mother! I should've been there for you, for Jerry, for your mother! But, please, please don't turn your back on me, now! You don't owe me forgiveness; you don't owe me time; you don't owe me love; you don't owe me anything, but please, please, Jenny, don't walk away from me now." Those were the words I had been waiting to hear for ten years.....and I couldn't walk away again; I couldn't go, so I stayed.......

December 23, 1998

Dear Diary,

It's been five days, since I first saw my father in the park and I must admit it's been pretty shaky. The first couple of days I was very reserved around him, like a shy kindergartener on the first day of school, but I could see in his eyes every time I saw him that he was trying, begging, pleading to see me again. He would constantly call my secretary at work and when she wasn't in, he would leave messages with anybody he possibly could. I tried to ignore him for a couple of days to get

**109**

my feelings together but when Eduardo, the janitor that cleans
up after closing at the gallery and the last person there, told
me that my father called for me one morning, I decided to
meet him for lunch that day. I mean...who was I kidding? I
knew I had unanswered questions that I was curious about; I
knew there was more I wanted to know about my father's
feelings about Jerry, about my father's feelings for my mother,
and about...him.


We spent the past few days getting to know each other
again and I tried my best to put the past in the past (no
matter how hard a task it was) and really tried to at least be
friends with my father. I hadn't worked up the courage to tell
Mark about John. I mean, Pa - until we had been seeing each
other for a couple of days. I haven't called my mother, because
she would probably go into a state of rage and call me a
traitor. This is probably the longest she has gone without
hearing from me and it helps that she's in Aspen with my aunt
and I probably won't even hear from her until Christmas Day.
On the other hand, Mark was supportive but protective and I
could understand why. Coming back after ten long years, there
was really no telling what my father could have wanted. But
really, as the days have been going, I am beginning to believe
that the only thing my father wants from me is my love
again...and I can't say...I can't say that I won't give it to him.


I'm supposed to pick him up at the hotel he is staying at
tomorrow; he wants to take me shopping in Times Square. It's

Christmas Eve and he said it will be like old times in a new age. I guess I'll just have to wait and see...


Jenny


The next day, I woke up bright and early to get an early start. I had done my Christmas shopping, weeks before and I told Mark I would come by his apartment to spend the night after my 'date' with my father; he was very understanding. I can't say the same for Whitney, my secretary; when I told her to take messages for all my calls for the day because I would be out with my father, she seemed to have almost spit her coffee out, before she asked me to repeat what I said. Her reaction made me laugh, as I wrapped my scarf tighter around my neck and made my way out of my apartment. I caught a cab over to my father's hotel and before I could let the past few days dawn on me too much (or bring me to tears), I was already there and was asking the woman at the front desk which room he was staying in.


"I'm sorry; there's no John Dawson staying here," the little woman with the petite voice said. Immediately, I thought something had gone wrong or that my father had checked out early.

"There must be some kind of mistake. Did he already check out?" I'm sure the woman could see the concern in my eyes, as she quickly explained that a John Dawson had never even checked into the hotel. I thanked her and walked briskly out of there to make sure I had come to the right hotel. I had - The Pimberton - but there was still no sign of my father. I almost felt tears coming to my eyes, as I began to think that my father probably went back home without saying goodbye....or maybe that it was too much to handle to be spending Christmas Eve with his long-lost daughter after ten years....I didn't know what to think, but I was practically sobbing, when I plunged back into a cab on my way to Mark's. I left a note at The Pimberton, in case anyone heard anything from my father. But at that moment, I felt he had run out on me once again.....and more importantly, that he had let me down......

December 25, 1998

Dear Diary,

Today is Christmas Day and it is truly the best Christmas I've had in a long time. It isn't a special Christmas because I'm sitting in the cozy living room of my fiancée near a warm, toasty fire; it isn't because I am enjoying a nice cup of holiday Folgers, watching the delicate little pillows of snow fall unto the ground outside a fogging, frosted window; it's because I got the best gift I could have ever gotten, the only thing I've longed for and hungered for and needed for years....closure.

 

It really is a wonder how we all survive life, because even with it being so incredibly difficult to carry on, at times, we still manage to make it. For years, I felt a pain in my heart that was so excruciating and heart-wrenching I thought I couldn't bear it. Beneath all of my success and all of my accomplishments, there was still that little girl in Portland, scrunched up in a ball on the floor of her room, sobbing uncontrollably like a defenseless child – not knowing what to do, not knowing what to think. But, now I know everything I need to know; I know exactly what I should think. Now, after all of these years and everything I've been through, I can finally see that I will be all right.

 

Last night, I got a call from The Pimberton and when I picked up the phone and listened to what was said, my whole face froze and all I could do was stare at Mark when he asked what was wrong. I couldn't possibly bring myself to believe what the woman had just told me, but as I quickly took the phone into the next room, the tears still began to flow. I hung up almost immediately, sat on my fiancé's bed and bawled hysterically. I couldn't even hear him begging to come in or his pounding on the locked door of his room, because I can hardly explain how I felt.

*My whole body was in a state of shock, as the words seemed to replay in my head like a horribly broken record: "Ms. Dawson. I was calling in regards to a note you left with us at The Pimberton. I work at the front desk and I think you ought to have a seat. I was completely positive that a Mr. John Dawson never checked into this hotel - this year, that is. Um, actually, ma'am, there was a John Dawson who made a reservation for this hotel, last year, but although he seems to have canceled his reservation, I was able to access his credit card information and home address. I hope you don't consider this meddlesome, ma'am, but I thought since it was Christmas, I would do you a favor. I ran a search on all the John Dawson's in Portland, Oregon as of last year and...well, out of the few that did come up in the search, this particular one was the only one to fit the description. Unfortunately, ma'am, if we are both speaking of John Allen Dawson, father of Jennifer Anne Dawson and deceased son, Jerry Keith Dawson, husband of Mary Anne Dawson, we are speaking of the John Allen Dawson who has recently passed away on the eleventh of this month."*

*I could not even consider what she had told me...I just couldn't. I laid on that bed and just cried and I cried for even longer when I did a little research on my own and found that it was all true. I suppose I was in more shock than anything for the simple fact that the whole thing was....impossible. If my father had passed away, the only logical explanation was absurd but it did explain everything - why he had waited so long to find* me...everything. It was simple and was oh so clear to me then....

He had made plans to come see me, but he second-guessed himself at the last minute, cancelled the reservation, and stayed home, only to die from cirrhosis a year later, realize what he had done and try to make it right. My heart ached for what seemed like forever, when I realized that my father had carried all that in his heart - all that he had done - until his death. He came to me as a ghost, or a spirit that had made mistakes in his life and finally realized it, even if it was a little tardy. But, the point is...he came to me...

Mark had finally broken the door in, when I had been locked in the room for over three hours and wouldn't come out. When he finally got to me, I dropped into his arms and clung to him like I had gotten to hold my father again after ten years. I spoke to him like I had gotten to finally speak to my father after ten years, and I realized, just this morning, that it didn't matter that it took my father ten years and death, even, to come and make things right with me; the only thing that mattered was the fact that he came. After ten long years of my life wasted in pain, I was able to start over, able to not forget the past, but accept it and forgive, and I was able to live again.

What a merry Christmas...

Sincerely,

Jenny

"Pain is temporary. It may last a minute, or an hour, or a day, or a year, but eventually it will subside and something else will take its place. If I quit, however, it will last forever"

Lance Armstrong

## Don't Follow Me
On sacrifices...

"Oh, God, help me. I try and I try, but I'm getting
nowhere. It's not my fault. She doesn't deserve a mother like me.
I'm a failure. Please don't do this to me; don't do it to her. Please,
please!"

The prayer above was recited on a cold and dismal
Saturday night in the scarcely lit, two-bedroom apartment (the
size of one) of Clara Suede. Shoddy apartments were all too
familiar to this desperate soul, because of all the money she spent
on "worthless things." Of course, it couldn't have been too much
of her fault, judging by the life she lived way before she had
another person to care for. Her mother was a relatively insane
woman with four children, whom she beat on a daily basis.
Luckily Clara was the oldest and she got away; she ran away
shortly after her seventeenth birthday and she never looked back.
It haunted her all her life that she left her two sisters and brother
all alone in that eerie, old house in Mississippi with the crazy
woman she loathed so deeply, but it was all she could do to
hopefully find a better way of life for herself.

Unfortunately, her mother died of a failing heart shortly
after she escaped, so Ms. Suede's other siblings were dropped
into foster care and Clara never forgave herself, especially since
she wasn't doing too badly, herself, in her small apartment in the

Bronx, New York. That was until she couldn't keep her rent payments steady and was forced to move out. She was juggling three jobs and had nowhere to stay...until she met Paul Benton. Although Clara wasn't the most emotionally stable person, she was quite beautiful with her gorgeous chestnut hair that seemed to flow on for miles and the emerald green eyes that always glistened in the sunlight; it didn't take Mr. Benton too long to notice her, during one of her shifts at the diner. She served him coffee, eggs and a side of toast and a few months later, he served her a wedding ring to match.

If only the perfect life Clara got to experience after so much misery could've lasted longer than one pregnancy and a couple arguments, maybe she would've ended up a little better off – or at least enough to take care of her baby girl. She was precious and fragile and just as beautiful as her mother, but sadly enough, she would probably end up just like her mother, since her father decided to kick the both of them out of their stunning estate in the Hamptons. Clara was back on a bus with her things to start over, once again, at her father's house not too far from where Paul and she used to live. He didn't exactly accept her and her newborn with open arms - at least not for free. He hadn't seen Clara in years, since he ran out on her mother, so he certainly wasn't going to let her "mooch" off of him without paying rent, especially because she had a baby.

Clara was used to her father's bitterness by now, as that was all he showed before he abandoned his family years ago. It

118

was just such a tragedy that Clara had no idea of the challenge before her, moving in with a total stranger. They fought almost non-stop over the pettiest of trivial matters, and they agreed on almost nothing. Through it all, Clara managed to find a job at a local department store, working long hours and struggling to find a place for her baby to stay while she was at work since her father refused to do it.

She was unwavering and she felt that all of the struggling and heartache she had to experience was all worth it to come home and have that precious child in her arms and bathe it and feed it - even on the days that she didn't have enough for herself to eat - and care for it and hold it in her arms, just smiling like she never smiled before. That baby was the only being in her life that needed her and depended on her and couldn't get rid of her and loved her always and unconditionally. Hope Love Suede was the name she gave her beloved child and the name certainly explained two things Clara was in absolute need of. It was a special sight watching Clara take care of her child, late nights in the wintry, damp basement of her father's house; although her father could care less about the "little runt" of Clara's as long as his daughter made rent every month, which after a couple months' time, she didn't and was kicked out of yet another place of shelter. It was only a misfortune that this one happened to be of someone that was supposed to love and care for her, but could not be more relentless to his firstborn or her child.

*"Go to some free shelter for moms and kids. I don't care where you go, but get the hell outta my house!"* Those were the last words Clara's father shouted at her as he threw her bags out into the rain of the frosty New York night. As the little luggage she owned shattered unto the ground, she hustled to pick them up, still juggling Hope in her arms.

"How am I supposed to get there, huh Reggie?" Clara shouted through tears of agony that were shielded by the cold drops of rain falling unto her face.

"Run! That's somethin' that you've always been good at, if it was the *only* skill you had!" Reggie slammed the door on the two of them, making his way back into his cozy home that he was sure to keep for quite some time as Clara scrambled to pick up her bags and make her way down the street, not knowing where to go or if she would even have anything when she got there.

Soon it had stopped raining and Clara had been walking in the forty-five degree weather for about a half-hour. Her face was frozen still. She seemed like a mindless zombie, roaming the streets in need of a purpose or a way. She was crushed, broken and devastated beyond belief as she started to wish her heart would suddenly stop beating, simultaneously with her daughter's. She seemed to have forgotten Hope was even there in her arms, when suddenly a car stopped beside her. She was barely out of her father's neighborhood when her baby was crying and little did she know, the person in that 1987 blue Chrysler was her only hope for the night. Although her face did not show any emotion whatsoever, she was prepared to hear what whoever it was had to stay, once they had rolled down the window.

"Now I might be mistaken, but I'm not sure if you wanna be walkin' in this weather," an older woman said through the rolled down window, now sprinkled with rain.

Clara was almost in a state of shock from all that was happening, as tears still increasingly rolled down her almost solid cheeks and she hastily tried to find the words to respond to the woman. "I'm trying....I just...I need to get out of this neighborhood and maybe find a place to stay for the night for free. My daughter can't be out in this weather, I'm sure." Clara peeled back the drenched cotton blanket and showed Hope's fragile little face to the woman; her breaths were short and she was wailing, uncontrollably.

"My dear God," the woman gasped and covered her mouth, as a single tears escaped each of her worried eyes. "Please, please get in. I'll get your things."

The elderly woman hurried to put Clara's things in her car and soon the two of them were on their way. Clara was saying goodbye to yet another tragic chapter in her life and the old woman had absolutely no idea what was going on.

The two of them were on the freeway by the time Meredith - the older woman - looked in the her rear view mirror to see Clara holding her baby, looking just as frozen as an ice cube. "My name is Meredith. What's yours, darlin'?" Clara could tell almost instantly that the woman was from somewhere in the South with her big hair, red fingernails, and bright clothes on such a cold night, but it was the least of her worries, as she was practically glued to the seat of the loud, bustling car with her daughter stagnant in her arms.

"Clara." She barely whispered her name. All she wanted was for the nightmare she thought she was experiencing to be over.

"I-I-I won't ask ya what has happened to ya, as I can see that it must've been somethin' terrible, judgin' by your face; why, you look like you've seen a ghost!" Meredith started to chuckle, but she soon discovered that it wasn't the time for joking. She didn't know the exact details of it all, but she was surely beginning to see that whoever this girl was, she had been through far too much to even smile for the next two months – let alone, that night. "But, I must ask, if there's anything I can do for ya or anywhere I can take ya."

The last words her father said to her were ricocheting from one of her ears to the other, but Clara knew they were quite true. Her last resort for the present times was a shelter for unlucky or beaten mothers and children and it was just her luck that Meredith knew just where to go: Saint Mary's Home for Mothers and Children.

"Well, here we are, darlin'." Meredith turned around in her seat to see Clara still motionless in her place with nothing to say; the old woman didn't have any idea what to do since she was already trying so hard.

Clara's hand crept further up Hope's delicate body, as her eyes began to glaze over once again from everything that had happened. She felt distraught and torn, while the words slowly crept out of her mouth, "Thank you, Ms. Meredith. You've been such a help and I'll never forget all that you've done."

A warmer smile came to Meredith's lips as she kept her eyes fixed on Clara. "It was no trouble at all to help someone in need, darlin'. Let me help you with your bags and take you to the door."

Meredith did just that, and once Clara got to the door of the shelter still holding her baby, everything after seemed like a dream. It was as if she blocked out and forgot everything - getting checked into a room by one of the nuns, bathing herself while the nuns bathed Hope, having a hot meal, praying and lying in bed - everything. All she could remember was lying in bed, staring at the carriage that Hope was lying in and beginning to cry.

As she watched her baby girl sleep and breathe, totally calm and relaxed, totally clueless with respect to their situation, Clara couldn't help but to weep, because even though her little girl of almost a year didn't know what was coming to pass, she did. She knew the things she had spent all her money on were worthless and pitiful in the end, destroying her life, causing her to lose jobs, homes, and her sanity. She lay staring at Hope Love for quite some time, thinking of these things – all she had come from, all she was destined to endure - until she finally fell asleep herself.

That night of sleep was almost like a miracle for Clara - the way she could sleep so peacefully, knowing that she had a definite place to stay the next morning she was awoken; knowing that her daughter was going to be all right if only for the moment; knowing that she was safe; and very most importantly, knowing that at this time in her life, she just might actually have a *real* chance. All she could do was be thankful for her blessings and sleep oh so peacefully.

The next morning, Clara was awoken by the golden ribbon of light streaming into the window of her and her daughter's room. She stretched and yawned, but didn't take too long to notice a dainty and fragile sound. It sounded so light and delicate and beautiful that she was instantly drawn from her pillow, as she crept out of bed to discover that it was coming from the carriage provided by the nuns, the night before. She slowly strolled towards the carriage, a smile reaching her lips. Peering over the ledge of the baby bed, she could see just what was making the sound.

It was Hope, lying in her carriage, twisting and turning as she giggled and laughed of joy. This scene brought tears to Clara's eyes, as she embraced her daughter and rocked her in her arms, realizing she had never seen Hope so happy. Tears of her own joy rolled down her cheeks, her hand now stroking the precious baby's hair, as she still smiled and laughed. It was at that moment that Clara finally saw that her daughter and she could actually be experiencing a new life with new ways and new chances and a new slate for just the two of them - *just the two of them.* These words meant all too much to Clara, because there was no one to hurt them in any way or kick them out of their house or tell them they weren't good enough, or anything of the sort. It was just the two of them and Clara knew it would be that way for a long time, but the best thing about it was that that was just the way she liked it and she had a great feeling that her little girl did, as well.

Clara soon found that the happiness that her and her daughter shared that bright and beautiful morning was going to continue on for quite some time. They shared many smiles and laughs together, as their time in the shelter was always joyful and enjoyable. Soon, Clara even got a steady job and was saving up every penny she earned, after seeking help for the addictions with which she had so much trouble.

She managed to stay consistent on her job as a mail girl at one of the most prestigious marketing companies in New York. Only a few years later, she had been promoted so many times that she had finally become secretary to the Vice President of Sales of the million dollar company. The poor woman had gone from getting up every morning at four a.m. - getting her child squared away, preparing herself for work, rushing to catch the subway, practically jogging all the way to the office, working the longest hours you could imagine with hardly any breaks, being totally exhausted by the time she caught the bus all the way home just to get her daughter ready for bed without having the least amount of time for her own night's meal, and being so exhausted that she just plunged into bed only to awake to the same hectic schedule the next day - all the way to saving up enough money for a car and folding that long and dreary schedule in half.

Clara worked diligently on her job and by the time her daughter's fifth birthday was but a day away, she had walked away from the shelter for a couple years by then and was living in her own apartment just a few blocks from her work, downtown. Her daughter had attended pre-school in the shelter, but she was now only a short while from attending a private elementary school after her birthday. Hope was now so beautiful with long, brown hair just like her mother's, and eyes that reminded Clara so much of her own mother's. She also had Clara's nose and mouth. She spoke like Clara, walked like Clara, smiled like Clara; she even laughed like Clara. They were an interesting pair and they were happy, the most important thing to Clara and it would be the most important thing to this woman of the troubled past, forever.

This is what she was thinking of as she sat at the window of the nook of her beautiful apartment overlooking downtown New York. The sky was dark, yet full of brilliant, scintillating stars, shining and glistening in the onyx-like night sky. Hope was sleeping peacefully in the next room in her tiny, little bed that fit perfectly to her small and dainty body, and Clara was healthy and happy and proud of all she had come from and all she had done. And yet, that night at the window, she was crying. Her hands were folded, her head quaintly angled to the sky, and yet she was *crying*. Only her tears were not of sorrow, nor heartache, nor hurt, nor pain; these tears were of elation and joy that Clara had never experienced once in her troublesome life – tears that overwhelmed her in a way she had never felt before.

Her hands were folded and she was crying because she was praying to God, the only one she felt she had to thank. She thanked Him for her current situation and all the blessings He had bestowed upon her and her daughter. As the tears flowed justly to her night gown, she reminisced on everything that had occurred between her and her parents and she assured God, that regardless of the hard times, she had finally learned to forgive both of them. She thought of her daughter and thanked Him repeatedly for bestowing upon her the chance to better her daughter's life. She begged God that the "good life" the two of them were experiencing would last far longer than any other time, since it was so needed and important for the sake of her child. Lastly, she thanked Him for her daughter's happiness, more so than her own. And, as she closed her eyes, tears simultaneously escaping them, she said "Amen" before she tiptoed to her bed, satiated, content, and spent from a joy so magnificent.

"Blow out the candles, baby," Clara said to Hope. It was the next day, and Clara had made the cake for the small birthday party she had prepared for the two of them in their quiet, cozy, little home. Hope didn't have many friends because the two of them moved around so much, but the best friend Hope had, at the time, was her mother and she truly believed that was the best friend she could ever have and would ever need.

"Thank you, Mommy. This is the best birthday ever!" Hope shouted, casting her arms around her mother's neck and hugging her dearly, a smile beaming from her face just like the ones she used to have when she was a baby.

"And it's only the beginning of many, many more, sweety," Clara said, smiling. She knew she could never promise that everything was going to stay as perfect as it had seemed at that moment, but she knew that she would do everything in her power to keep it that way, as that was all she *could* do.

After that day, everything seemed to be going fine, but there *is* a particular day I feel I should mention; I do believe I should. It was Monday, so Clara got up a little earlier than usual. She headed to the bathroom, washed her face, brushed her teeth ...the usual schedule. Soon, Hope was up and they ate breakfast together before she took her to her new elementary school, as they did every other week day.

"Bye, Momma," Hope said, as the two of them stood outside the door of her classroom at Crescent Hills Elementary School, a private elementary school for gifted and talented children.

"Bye, sweety. Have a good day and be good." Clara leaned down to kiss her daughter and then watched her walk into the classroom.

"I will, Mommy."

Clara smiled at her little girl one last time, before she headed back out to her car. She was so proud to see that Hope was happy and doing exceptionally in her new school, but she knew if she didn't get going she would be late for work.

The streets of downtown were so crowded that Clara could barely get into the parking garage, but when she finally did. She dashed to the elevator and up to the twenty-second, before she was pronounced late.

As the elevator doors separated, she took a deep breath with a proud smile and tugged on her new, black, two-piece suit to tidy it. She took one step outside the elevator and thought she was prepared for anything, without a clue of what was in store for her that day. Clara smiled and waved as she passed all her co-workers at their cubicles; she haughtily passed all of them to get to her *nicer* office nearest her boss, Dan Wyatt.

She was happy to be there just as any other day at her office, but this time as she pranced into her office with her neat smile and outfit, she saw a sight that confused her and made her think twice about going all the way in; it was a few boxes lined up on her desk with her things inside. Taken aback, she couldn't find any words after gasping in complete shock.

Puzzled, Clara strolled to her boss's office and knocked before she let herself in. Dan was dressed in a nicer looking, *expensive* suit and was talking on the phone with what seemed to be a very important client from the company's very wide selection of important clientele. He held up a finger, meaning Clara would have to wait, something she really wasn't in the mood to do. She was already more anxious than she would've preferred to be so early in the morning.

She waited a couple minutes and by the time he finally ended his call, he looked straight at her and grinned expressively. "Good morning, Clara. Sit down; get comfortable."

"Oh, no, Mr. Wyatt, I won't be long. I just wanted to know if there was some cleaning or something to be done in my office. I couldn't help but notice all of the boxes aligned on my desk with my things in them." Clara tried to smile, but couldn't figure out how. There was too much to be explained and her heartbeat had already risen above its normal speed.

Dan Wyatt took a second to quickly stare at Clara. He folded his arms on his desk, neatly adjusting his position in his chair, "Please sit down, Clara."

Clara stood where she was for a moment trying to read the look in his eyes before she apprehensively and slowly made her way to one of the chairs placed before the desk of her boss. His face was as serious as she could've ever imagined when she quaintly and quietly pulled a chair from under the desk and primly sat in it, crossing her legs.

Mr. Wyatt paused for a moment before he spoke, as if he were trying to piece together the exact words he wanted to say to Clara, ignoring the fact that it was killing her to have to wait. "Clara, you know you've been my secretary and assistant for some time now." He rubbed his chin and went on, "Do you think your stay here at Clifton International has gone well?"

Clara wasn't sure she should answer right away or what she should have said at that point, but she came to her senses and answered, "Well, I would say it has." She nervously laughed and went on, "I come to work on time every day, work hard, and leave at night. I get my check on time every week; I would say that's pretty good."

"Good, then, you can agree that you should move on to find new and better things – even better work experiences." Mr. Wyatt sat back, propped his feet up on his desk and smiled, as he placed his hands in his lap. He had no idea just what he was doing to Clara, but by then, Clara was beginning to believe that he didn't care, either.

She was so confused and her face was beginning to show it. "What do mean, Mr. Wyatt? I don't understand..."

Dan leaned up again in his dark brown imported leather chair, placing his arms on the desk once again as he said, "I'm saying, Clara, you know how I am about new and fresh things - new cars, new clothes, new clients, new business deals, new...secretaries."

Right when he said that, Clara became speechless, as she felt tears beginning to instantly build up in her eyes. She finally began to understand the boxes on her desk in her office and her boss's unwanted candidness.

Dan didn't even let what he had just said sink in before he proceeded to unknowingly tear her to even smaller shreds. "Think of it as a vacation, Clara. You just don't come back."

Ms. Suede was so shocked by her boss's uncanny expression, his ruthlessness, his subtle way of firing her. She didn't know what she had done wrong; she didn't know what to think or feel or do, so she just left, before he could see the large tears that were just fiercely yearning to cascade from her eyes.

Short Stories

As she hastily rushed down the carpet floor and passed all
the people in the cubicles she felt she was higher than, she could
hear her boss shouting at her, "It didn't have to end this way!"
and things of the sort. But, Clara knew, at that time in her life,
that it did have to end that way, just as tragically as many of the
other plentiful, yet depressingly short times in her life.

As she rode in the elevator all alone, she cried with all her
might, and once she had reached her car, she could barely get the
key into the ignition, because of the great pain now growing in
her stomach. Once she got on the road, she couldn't take it
anymore, so she pulled over to cry as she truly needed to. She
grasped her stomach in her hand, as memories of her past
mistakes and more bad luck flashed before her eyes. She couldn't
bear it, and began crying harder than she ever cried, with a pain
that seemed to make her whole body ache. What would she do
with her life now that she had to basically start over? How would
she explain the situation to her daughter? What was she going to
do? These were all the questions that quickly drifted through her
mind, as her head rested on the steering wheel of her car and her
hair fell over her damp face of tears.

Clara's eyes merely caught a glimpse of the red numbers of
the current time, gleaming from her dashboard; her vision was
fogged by the tears streaming out of her eyes, but she could
certainly see that it was 9:32. The next time she saw the time was
when she was awakened by the sun starting to fade, after crying

135

herself to sleep and staying that way for much longer than she intended.

As the clock struck 3:22, she hurried as fast as she could - with an aching body, torn soul and cold face from the tears she had cried for some time - to crank her car and get to her daughter's school in time to pick her up.

It was all a blur to her - getting to the school - but for only an instant, nothing else seemed to matter, as she stood outside her daughter's classroom and gazed inside. The class hadn't let out yet, so she found herself sullenly staring at her daughter playing amongst the other children; she seemed to be having the most fun Clara had seen her have in quite some time. Feeling a tear slowly stream from her eye, Clara smiled, but couldn't help the overwhelming feeling of sadness within – the unnerving pang of uncertainty from fright of what could possibly happen to her daughter's life now that she had no income to support her. The tears began to collect on her blouse as she envisioned having to steal her daughter away from everything she had worked so arduously to provide her with and the beautiful life she had *finally* been able to promise her.

It was getting even harder to hide her grief once Hope had been in her mother's view for more than a few hours. The car ride home, dinner, and doing homework was harder than ever for

Clara. It was an effort to avoid bursting into tears just from looking at her daughter's precious little face, because it reminded her of how much of a failure she was and how much she had let her daughter down.

"Mommy, what's wrong?" Hope stood in front of the open door of her mother's room, holding her favorite teddy bear in her arms. She was ready for bed and had come to ask Clara to read her a story or talk to her about her day, as they usually did. But even at the tender age of five years old, Hope knew tonight was not going to be the night to hear "Goldilocks" or talk about the house of cards she helped her best friend, Taylor build in class that day. The poor little one froze in front of her mother's door with silent, yet compassionate curiosity in her face, because her mother was leaning over her bed crying in the dark.

Clara leaned up from the bed and quickly wiped her tears of distress. "Nothing, baby. Nothing's wrong. What makes you think I was crying?" Clara nervously forced out a laugh, as she walked towards her daughter to sweep her into her arms.

"You *were* crying, Mommy; I saw you." The bright little girl's voice was so serious and definite as she said it and her mother carried her to her room.

"I wasn't crying, honey; Mommy wasn't crying. What story do you wanna hear, tonight?" Clara changed the subject to avoid any more questions. She couldn't bear the thought of telling her daughter what had really happened and how it might affect her, partly because she, herself, was afraid of how awful and excruciating the real truth could be.

Despite everything that had occurred, Clara still found herself reading Mary Poppins in the cozy, little pink room of her daughter, as the two of curled up together in the rocking chair Clara had bought just for such occasions. She peacefully read the story and stroked her long hair away from her pretty little face.

"Hope, honey…" Clara could feel a ball swelling up in her neck, as her nose turned red and Hope played with the necklace Clara was wearing.

"Yes, Mommy?" Hope felt herself yawn, as Clara closed the book.

"You know I love you and I would do anything for you, don't you, baby?" Clara could feel herself beginning to cry, but she felt she had to hold her tears back with all she had left.

"Yes, Mommy."

"I would sacrifice my all for you, Hope. I would." A stubborn tear began to overwhelm her, so she quickly whisked Hope to her bed and put her under the covers.

Luckily for Clara, the child had already fallen asleep, so she leaned down to kiss her on her cheek. It was a kiss that lasted some time and expressed her undying and unconditional love for her only child – the child she had only wanted the best for and had only continued on in her own life to provide for, the child who miraculously delivered her from her past and unknowingly provided her with an ultimate sense of joy that she carried with her in her every movement, the child, whom she would do anything just to insure herself that she would be everything she never was and so much more. The tear she had so persistently held back, soon fell right unto Hope's little fragile baby face. Clara gently wiped it away, hoping that her baby girl would never forget the meaningful words she had just shared with her from the bottom of her broken heart. At that defining moment – watching her child slowly fall into a deep, naïve slumber - she made a promise to herself that even if her daughter forgot the words, she would never foolishly bring herself to forget them for anything in the world.

That night was somewhat of a turning point in Clara's life, much for the benefit of herself and, ultimately, her daughter. The next few days were easier to withstand, as Clara began to find different ways to obtain money from the government after receiving her last check from the editing office. Her daughter stayed at her school for as long as Clara could scrounge up the money to afford it, something that seemed to last only a moment. One bright Friday morning, after weeks of tirelessly working to raise money to afford the thousand-dollar-a-month institution, Clara received a call from the dean of Crescent Hills saying the school would have to "...remove Hope from the program for lack of payment." Instantly, she collapsed into a state of depression, just as the phone fell unto the plush carpet of her apartment floor.

From then on, things only seemed to get worse and worse and Clara had finally decided to come clean to her daughter about what had really been happening to the two of them; she could barely bring herself to say the words, after her daughter asked, "Why are they taking me out of my school, Mommy? All my friends are there and I love it."

All Clara could do was turn her head, fighting the undying urge to cry like she had been doing for weeks upon weeks. "Honey, Mommy is going through a rough time, so the school has decided to help us and let you go to another school that isn't so expensive."

Unfortunately that was the first of many "little white lies" that Clara had to tell her five and a half year old. When there wasn't enough food in the house, it was "The grocery store was closed today"; when Hope couldn't get her favorite toy, it was "Toys aren't that important, honey"; when the light bill came and the service was terminated, it was: "The power company cuts the lights off in some homes to keep the energy flowing evenly through the city, Honey; it'll be all right." Every time there was a problem, Clara came up with a different lie, a different excuse, and a different way to disguise the fact that she wasn't making it. Clara felt she couldn't do it by herself. She felt alone, scared, and most importantly, defeated. All that was left in her heart was depression, lost dreams, and failed hope – nothing more, nothing less.

After struggling with bills, school payments, and even more money issues, Clara looked back on the past six months, after her daughter's sixth birthday came to pass, and had discovered that her daughter and she had moved a total of four times. The two of them went from an upscale, luxury apartment in downtown New York City to one of the roughest neighborhoods in the state of New York. Sooner than later, Hope stopped asking about the bills, water, electricity, her school, or anything else that she knew was going wrong, because she had quickly become used to it all - used to the fact that there was no food to eat, used to the fact that there was no new school clothes to wear, used to the fact that her and her mother were a part of the "poor people," as she might tell her friends at school.

The most tragic issue of Clara's new life "transformation" was that she had faded back to her old life style of depression and the scapegoats so heavily mentioned. She was crying the most she had ever cried in her life. She became consumed with guilt and pain, as her life seemed to merely drift by her as well as the life of her daughter. Her helplessness and failure lurked in her mind all hours of the day and she couldn't look at herself in the mirror for the fear that she would only burst out in tears towards the image of the person she had become. She couldn't eat, she couldn't sleep, and she felt as if she were engulfed in a horrifying nightmare, begging and pleading to be awoken.

This leads us back to where we began. Clara feebly perched on her knees and prayed the prayer so many pages ago. The words came to her as a surprising whisper with a delivery weaker than the minute strength she had left. The 'worthless things' of heroine, alcohol, cigarettes, and cocaine scattered across the floor suddenly became a vague reality, as she sat on the matted carpet floor of her small bedroom in her trashy apartment, glaring at the past two month's bills, rent notices, and food stamps beneath the syringes piled on top of them. Absolutely spent, her sanity was slowly drifting away from her; her body was worth less than the pack of Camel's she had just finished off. She had no money; she was addicted to drugs that were costing her *everything* she had left to prize; she had reached her limit with no urge or incentive to look back at the past that had caused her so much heartache or dare to envision the future that she no longer saw for herself alive to see and feared for the sake of her daughter. All she had left in her life was her daughter - her beautiful baby girl that she had put through so much, but was the most important possession she could've ever asked for.

She realized at that moment that she didn't want fancy clothes, or apartments, or anything of a materialistic state. All she ever wanted was a better life than she ever had herself for her only child.

"Mommy," was all Hope could say when she hesitantly strolled into her mother's room and saw her body filthy, the mess on the floor, and her mother's eyes full of tears.

Clara took a deep sigh and didn't even bother to wipe away her tears or hide the muddle of depressants before her, as she slowly reached her arms out for her daughter and pulled her close. Once Hope was in her arms, her little fragile face nestled to her mother's chest, she began her confession, something she owed that beautiful little girl for quite some time. "Honey...you know Mommy hasn't been the most honest person with you, baby. I've lied to you about our home and our situation for a while and I was wrong. You're not old enough to understand now, but you will, one day..."

"Mommy, what do you mean?" Hope began to cry, frightened by the huge black circles around her mother's eyes and her trembling hands, but Clara only pulled her closer and went on.

"I want what is best for you. I want you to be okay, baby...I don't like for you to see me this way and I promised you, only a little while ago, that everything would be okay and I'm going to keep my promise. Okay, honey?" Clara's face was as frozen as Oregon forests in the winter – her heart slowly beating and her mind as blank as the pages of an untold story. The tears in her eyes were like icy droplets of rain, splashing onto Hope's little head.

"Okay, Mommy; please don't cry. I don't want you to be sad anymore." Hope so nobly hugged her mother tighter than she had ever hugged her and just sat in her arms, bewildered and forlorn.

The two of them sat in each other's arms and cried long and meaningfully for a countless amount of time, until Hope fell asleep in her place and for a moment, Clara sat breathless and torn. She slowly took her baby girl's clothes off and replaced them with a night gown, and laid her in her bed. Then, she went to Hope's room, looking around at all of her playthings and her tiny little bed, regressing on everything that had occurred in the last few months and in the poor child's life. Everything cascaded upon her heart and delivered her a relentless sense of guilt and undying pain; out of a fit of sorrowful rage and resentment, she decided to pack. She packed all of her daughter's clothes and the few favorite toys she had left, and her favorite coloring books and crayons and her little hair bows and her little Mary Jane shoes.

Clara shoved everything into any piece of luggage or bag she could find in the child's room, as her tears stained some of the clothing or stuffed animals, and when the last bag was packed, she leaned over it and cried incessantly until she couldn't conjure up a single breath from her lungs. A powerful migraine pulsated through every vain in her troubled head, as she knew what she had to do. It all came to her as if it were an omen from heaven and she knew what she owed her daughter - it was something she had owed her from birth, even. She felt it to the very core of her being and kept it with her, as she slowly walked back to her room and quietly and gently lay beside her daughter, stroked her pretty hair, and held her close and slept with her and loved her with all her heart, all she had left to give. "I love you, sweetie and I'm going to give you what you deserve, no matter how hard it is going to be. I love you, my baby. I love you, Hope," She whispered through her tears all through the night.

The next morning, Clara was up earlier than the sun. She pensively and gradually made her daughter's favorite breakfast, seeming to absorb every moment of the morning, especially when Hope appeared.

"Good morning, Mommy." Hope quietly yawned, not knowing what that bright morning had in store for her.

"Good morning, hun; go get washed up. There's an outfit on your bed for you to wear." Clara spoke softly, as she could barely speak. She was afraid to say too much, for the pain seemed to flow through her every word.

"Okay, Mommy." Hope turned to do what her mother had asked of her, as Clara watched her little pink night gown disappear into the other room. She looked out the window and tears immediately fell from her eyes. She allowed a small shrill to come from her mouth and she was glad Hope wasn't there to hear it.

Soon, the two of them were dressed and had eaten breakfast together. The whole time, Clara couldn't keep herself from rubbing her daughter's head or staring into her pretty little face, as she barely ate, thinking of all the moments they shared together – just the two of them. But, soon, it was time for her to take the first step towards the most heart-breaking thing she knew she would ever have to do.

As she loaded Hope's things unto the bus they were taking, Hope asked many times where the two of them were going, but Clara's only answer was, "Be patient, baby; you'll see." There was a certain calmness in her heart, which didn't help the tears from falling, as she peered out the window of the bus.

The bus soon stopped outside of a place Clara thought she would never have to take her daughter. She quickly grabbed

Hope's things and took her inside of the building, trying to avoid any more agony than she was already experiencing. Hope's questions persisted, when Clara and she sat in the waiting room, but she desperately attempted to ignore her. Even after Clara signed sufficient paperwork, she tried wholeheartedly to ignore the little girl's eyes - the eyes she had loved since she had brought her daughter into the world, the same eyes that had brought her so much joy and the first sense of accomplishment she had ever encountered, and the same eyes that, at that moment brought her so much heartache and a twinge in her soul that she would never forget.

A woman there to assist children in this place, looked happily at Hope's beautiful face and said, "Welcome to your new home, honey. I'm Harriet and I'm gonna be your new friend."

"This is where we're going to live, Mommy?" Hope asked - her eyes full of excitement; she had always liked adventures, but that same look brought Clara to even fresher tears, as she was finally forced to face the naïve child.

Clara mournfully looked her daughter straight in the eye and answered, now crying the heaviest tears she had cried all morning and all of her life. "No, baby; this is where you're going to live. This is Albany Court Adoption Home. These people are going to take care of you until you can get a new home...without Mommy."

"Mommy, I don't understand. Why can't you stay?" Hope's enthusiasm quickly turned into a tragic pain of her own feeling and undeniable fear. Harriet watched and began to cry herself.

Clara searched for the words to say, but there were none. She was leaving her baby – she was leaving her in this place, turning her back, and walking out on the little one that had been the only love of her life, since Paul. She was abandoning her for life and that was it. "Baby, you know I love you..."

"I know, Mommy; I just want you to stay! I'll miss you if you go." Hope burst out in tears and threw her arms around Clara's waist, as she pleaded as hard as she could for her mother, her best friend, her hope, her everything, to stay.

"Honey, I can't take care of you. As much as I love you and care for you, your staying with me hurts me and it hurts you, too. I cannot provide for you the way I want to and Mommy didn't have a good life and you'll never understand, but it's not your fault. I promised you I would do what's best for you and I would sacrifice for you and this is doing what I promised. You know Mommy loves you with all her heart; don't you?" Clara was crying just as her daughter was and as she said the words, she found herself beginning to truly believe them to be true.

"So, let me show you," she kneeled to look Hope in her beautiful, bright eyes, submerged in tears. "I want you to be good and respect these people and grow up to be a wonderful person and live a beautiful life and be better than me. You're my angel and my princess and I'm not leaving you; I'm with you every night when you go to sleep and every day, when you wake up. You hear me, Hope?" Clara said with all her strength, as she realized she *was* doing the right thing.

Hope nodded once again, and Clara went on after a long pause of thought and emotions and feelings she had never experienced. "I love you, baby, but I'm telling you, when you see me walk out that door, please, baby, please...don't follow me."...*Don't follow me*...a few words that had quite a few meanings when said by this mother to her child, but the most important connotation they held was do not fall prey to the lifestyle I live - the mistakes I have made, the wrong I have done, and the heartache I have caused. Don't follow me down this lonely road of destruction and tears and hurt. *Don't follow me.*

Hope cried so hard as her mother kissed her forehead and hugged her for the last time. When Clara walked out the door without looking back, hearing her daughter cry and scream for her to come and get her, she realized that she had to keep walking; she knew in her heart that she had finally done the right thing for the sake of her only child...

"There can be no high civility without a deep morality."

Ralph Waldo Emerson

## Peace in the Snow
On values....

Donna Jensen always had a love for a toasty evening dinner by an open fire in a small and quiet place during the winter. To her, it didn't really matter where the place was, as long as it was a rendezvous to relax and escape the busy and cluttered, yet profitable life she lived. As a gorgeous, intelligent, intuitive, and suave editor in the big city of Los Angeles, California, it was a far cry from the small town in the mountains where she was raised. Juggling coffee and half-baked stories written by new journalist hopefuls of the writing realm and hardly being able to schedule a decent lunch for herself, would have to be fairly different from long rides back and forth from her home to town in the winter with her father, in her younger years. These times she missed dearly and thought of them often as she sat at her pine oak desk on floor thirty-five on Thursday morning, shuffling through a pile of articles dropped off by one of her co-workers just a few hours before.

Flipping through each page, she thought of the dinners her mother would make for her and her father after a long day of work, cutting logs and selling goods in town. By the time a small smile could reach her lips she was interrupted, yet again, by her assistant, who had somehow managed to scrape up a bit of coffee and some telephone messages from that morning.

With a single knock, she let herself in and began to say quite a few things to Donna - as she always did - but Ms. Jensen never had a problem with this habit of Martha's, since she reminded her very much of one of her family's closest neighbors in the mountains. It made her smile again, as she kindly asked her secretary to repeat what she had just said.

"I'm sorry to bother you, Ms. Jensen, but I brought you your morning coffee and a few messages. A lady over at Vogue wants to speak with us about an article we released last Wednesday - a Jennifer Caldwell - and said that three of the designers for this week's cover were fired and need to be replaced. Also, a Peter Harrison called about some cabin in the mountains; he said it was really important and he needed to speak to you as soon as possible." By the time the speedy lady had finished telling Donna the news, she had already set the coffee and the list of telephone numbers from the messages on her desk.

Ms. Jensen simply thanked her assistant and let her make her way out of her office, as she just sat at her desk, lingering on the last words her assistant had said: *"Peter Harrison called about some cabin in the mountains; he said it was very important and he needed to speak to you as soon as possible."* She had

heard phrases like this before, used by many of the
people from the town she lived in as a child. It just so
happened that the cabin her parents owned, until their
death only five years before, was one of the nicest cabins
in the town, especially because it was the highest on the
mountain. It was a very nice cabin of the finest wood and
antique fixtures, but the people of the town particularly
loved it because it was just as the rumor had it: the first
house to get snow. But that was why Donna loved it so
much; the cabin meant more to her than money or gifts
or compliments. It was the place she was raised and had
spent some of her best moments; it was the place her
parents spent most of their young life and also the last
place they saw before their deaths. Donna was
determined not to sacrifice this cabin for any amount of
money - no matter how much it was.


    Ms. Jensen quickly noticed, after calling Peter
Harrison and speaking to him for a short time, that he
was prepared to offer a very large sum of money for the
cabin - such a large amount that it almost startled
Donna and led her to ask him for more time to think
about the matter. They ended the conversation briefly,
but the issue was on Donna's mind for the rest of the
day.


    During the car ride home, she thought of her
parents and the time they shared in the cabin - how

beautiful, yet simple the times were, how full and warm the house felt, compared to her lonely, yet very expensive, condo amongst the busy downtown streets of LA. It was filled with nineteenth century paintings and pottery, antique furniture and all wood floors, but it felt nothing like her home in the mountains. The smell of her home was of a chemical-based pine oil, but it only reminded her of the real smell of pine wood she would encounter, walking into her old cabin home, as the frost from the outside caught up with her body, just in time to feel the heat of the fire blazing in the fireplace.

It was almost a dream thinking of all of this, as Donna stepped out of the shower, twirled a robe around her waist, and made her way to her vanity mirror and stool, where she began to brush her long brown hair. She looked just like her mother and it almost shamed her to think of just what her mother would think if she traded the cabin for money that she could make in a few months' time on her job in LA. Donna hung her troubled head at the thought, threw a night gown over her head, leaving her robe on the stool, as she climbed into bed after the lights were turned off.

The poor woman would've been distressed about the topic at hand if a small gust of crisp air from her open window hadn't frosted her nose, making her think of a very bright idea: she could spend one last weekend at the cabin to make her final decision. It would be just about first snow in her old town and even if she decided not to keep the cabin, it would be the perfect ending to the magical fairy tale the cabin had created for her and her family.

Donna could hardly sleep thinking of the next morning that indeed quickly arrived. She could hardly prevent anxiousness as she called in for a few days away from work and for her assistant to take messages for all her calls, after which she packed all her best sweaters, scarves, and coats, grabbed a steaming hot thermos of hot chocolate, and rushed out of her condo door, almost forgetting to lock it.

Standing in line at the train station, drinking the hot chocolate, Donna felt like a girl again, eagerly waiting to buy a ticket to see a best friend or relative she hadn't seen in what seemed to be ages, and it had been. After purchasing her ticket, Donna was soon on her way to the town and cabin she had missed so dearly and had caused her some trouble to keep in her life, but had also given her great joy.

Perched upright in the train seat, she could feel the rocky path beneath the wheels of the speedy train and see the beautiful scenery of tall pine trees and clear skies above, while the frostiness of the outside glazed the window in a delicate and effortless manner. She envisioned the door handle of the cabin in the palm of her hand, once she had reached the town. She closed her eyes to see the entire town before her as she sat in her seat and Donna wondered just how magnificent it would be to be back in the place that she loved so much.

Soon this feeling of pure delight would be of her possession, as the train came to a stop in the small mountain town. Ms. Jensen's heart jolted inside of her as her hands grasped the bar in front of her and she rose to her feet to take her bags and make her way to the front of the train. The other passengers crowded off also, but when her foot hit the ground off the train steps, it felt as if time had stopped and all before her was a wonderful dream that she never wanted to wake up from. As the cold and frigid air hit her cherry red nose, she took a deep breath and opened and closed her eyes to clutch every second of the moment before her.

She could hardly wait to make her way up the mountain and before she knew it she was hiking up the mountain with her guide. The almost dazed woman hardly said a word to the man as he tried to make conversation with her, missing the fact that she was full of anxiousness - every second increasing it more and more. The man didn't know how long Donna had waited to see this place so near and dear to her, but as soon as they reached the cabin and he saw the expression on her face, he discovered what he had been missing. As the sun shone in her eyes, he saw a stare of great amazement and splendor, accompanied by the excitement flowing through her face.

Donna hadn't been to this beautiful place since her parents passed away, but it looked exactly the same. She had barely said goodbye to the man and paid him when she found out that the inside was just as magical as she had remembered. Dropping her bags briskly to the floor, she almost cried when she walked through every room in the house, running her hands on every familiar window sill, wall, and picture frame - all the memories of the cabin running back to her faster than a gazelle in the Sahara. The instant was so overwhelming, but beautiful as she quickly arrived at the room that was most important to her: her room from childhood. Her mother was so sweet to leave every picture, doll, blanket, sheet, and figurine just the same as it was when she was just fourteen years old. A tear rolled from her eye as she looked at this sight of simple love presented by a simple room that made her feel so warm and whole inside.

Ms. Jensen left her name in the city and now she was just Donna, sitting in front of an open fire in her mother's old rocking chair, wrapped in her mother's old handmade quilt, sipping tea and flipping through old letters from other townspeople trying to buy the cabin from her. She quickly tossed them on the coffee table next to her as she tried to feel her mother's arms wrapped around her the same way they used to be when she was a child. She tried to feel her father's eyes on her, watching in pure love and admiration. It felt so wonderful to be home - to cook in her mother's kitchen, to sleep in the bed her father had made with his own bare hands, to rock in her mother's antique rocking chair given to her by her own mother, to be in the presence of the place once so complete and warm and comforting at all the right moments. Donna fell asleep in her old bed, peaceful and satiated as a small child, and didn't awake until morning.

The frost from the next day awoke Donna as she yawned and slowly rose out of bed just as she used to, only back then her mother would wake her. For some reason it felt as if her parents were there as she washed and dressed for the day. It almost felt like her father was waiting with her for breakfast from her mother, after Donna had just ordered the groceries from town. When they arrived, she made her favorite breakfast of pancakes, eggs, hash browns, and hot chocolate, using her favorites of her mother's recipes. She yearned so deeply for her mother and father to be eating with her at the table and each bite reminded her of the breakfasts they would share together – breakfasts full of smiles and laughs, moments that would always be cherished.

Swept away in her memories, she had just finished her meal when a miraculous thing took place. A sight so unreal, Donna couldn't wait to see, as she almost slammed her mug down to scurry to the window for something she had been waiting for, ever since she had gotten to town the day before - a gorgeous and simple expression of the astonishing beauty of the beloved family cabin and the town...the first snow. It was just as the rumors had said: she was the first to see these small and delicate balls of frosty ice, dazzling in the little sun fading away into the sky, cascading upon the roof of the cabin and flowing down the slopes of the mountain like a tide of everlasting white diamonds streaming by the stroke of the wind.

It was a sight that made her decision for her; she instantly decided she couldn't sell the cabin - she couldn't sell it because of the memories, the love, the warmth, the comfort, the shelter it provided. It was her father's masterpiece given to her mother and herself, a place to call home for so many years - so many years that they watched this blanket of white purity fall during every winter, as her family and she huddled up inside. It was a place to escape the troublesome and hectic life she lived, once she left the cabin as an older teenager.

In that *little* cabin in the mountains of that *little* town in the middle of nowhere special, she knew she had a place to forget her problems and take on new adventures of joy, merriment, and happiness. Looking out the window at the striking scene of serenity, she discovered something she would never get in the city and that was peace...in the snow.

*Short Stories*

"He who floats with the current, who does not guide himself according to higher principles, who has no ideal, no convictions – such a man is a mere article of the world's furniture – a thing moved, instead of a living and moving being – an echo, not a voice."

Philosopher Henri Frederic Amiel

## Short Stories

### Rain Rain Go Away
On morals...

*Pitter patter pitter patter drip drop drip drop* ...This was
the sound of the rain on the roof of 114 Rockerdelle Lane,
commonly known as Heavenly Blessings Adoption Home for
Underprivileged Children, in a small town just outside of
London. This was such a beautiful sound and a treat to hear
throughout the long halls of the home, even as early in the
morning as it was – not because of the sound of the rain itself,
but because of the sweet and calming sound of a tiny little girl's
very *big* voice accompanying the rain, streaming throughout
every room. She was singing her favorite song to sing at her
favorite time: when it was raining. How beautiful her voice
sounded, how beautiful such a simple and generic thing such as
singing "Rain Rain Go Away" could sound. It wasn't the sound
of the song that made it so beautiful; it was where it came from –
an interesting, little child that had been through so much, yet still
found it in her heart *to sing*. I presume I should tell you about
this little girl that, now, to you, may seem quite fascinating and
definitely has a story worth telling.

The day this little girl was born was the day one of the
most prestigious doctors in her town was awestruck more than he
had ever been in all the thirty-two years he had been in practice.

**165**

The expression on his face was pretty much the look of everyone in the room when the poor little baby girl emerged from her mother's womb. You might understand that this little one was a healthy baby, all in all; she had clear skin, the perfect soft hair of a new-born, beautiful brown eyes, and a cry that made her mother smile, until her mother saw her...ears. The fragile and precious little girl was born with one enlarged ear. Although she was as gorgeous as a little girl could be, she wasn't gorgeous enough for her mother, the governor's wife. Her mother had the best of friends, cars, clothes, jewelry and many other things, including her husband, and had her heart set on the most impeccably perfect daughter to match. So you can imagine how she felt when her "little bundle of joy" was born.

"How could my daughter come out this way? As beautiful as you are...how could this be, Matilda?" the governor asked his wife, scratching his head and, distraughtly peering into the carriage of his baby girl the night after the birth.

Mrs. Grennom's hair was unraveled in the most wretched manner, as she had been grabbing and scratching at her head, trying to figure out how it all had happened. She was a perfectly healthy woman of a slender and narrow shape, her mother and father were healthy, and their parents were healthy. She certainly was confused about the whole predicament. She displayed her disgust in the most appalled face you would think you had ever seen as she turned away from her daughter, casting her arms into the air.

Matilda wept briefly, as she had in mind what she would *have* to do because, after all, the baby was her own flesh and blood, emotions, and had been her every thought and cause of anxiousness for the past nine months she had carried her. "Oh, Robert. Look at her; we simply cannot have this! I've heard of babies like this turning into a swan, but as of now she looks like the ugly duckling!"

*The ugly duckling*...the forlorn mother said, and it quickly became the little girl's nickname. The confused little infant was quickly bundled up in a silk wrap, whisked into a black limo, appointed a skilled driver of the governor's mansion, and driven away to a place, from which the little baby would never return, never to 'burden' her parents again. Just as quickly as you could say "The End," this little duckling's story began...

"What is the case, ma'am?" a woman at the front desk of this place asked the *other* woman appointed to see to it that the baby was well-placed. The older woman was the assistant of the governor's wife with a  wider frame, gray hair, and a pencil nose that even more so added to her strict and disgustingly unconcerned attitude. (She might have even been a little more ruthless than the infant's parents were acting; the only difference was the fact that *this* assistant actually intended to be this way.)


The assistant - Ms. Blanchard - took one last sickened look at the governor's child, turning her nose in the air at the baby's face, and said, "*It* is - well, I'll keep their names confidential for the sake of their reputation – but whose *it* is should be of no concern, lady. She was just born today and they don't want her. I can't say I blame them, because if you were to have one good look at her head, you would know for yourself the reason that is as clear as day itself."


"Yes, ma'am; I understand. And...her name?" The patient nun had instantly become concerned for the child and developed a sense of pity for it, as she tried to get somewhat of a good look at the baby.

Ms. Blanchard was well past prepared to just drop the baby on the counter of the nun's desk, but after a quick and uncouth laugh, answered, "I'm surprised they actually gave the thing a name, actually, but after all, it is the old bloke's daughter. But, anyhow, her name was dreadful, indeed, but I believe they decided on Delia Lucille Grennom."

"Yes, ma'am and I will take her now, if you'll just sign here and leave sufficient information for me to contact the parents." The nun reached her hands out for Delia and was made even more uncomfortable by Ms. Blanchard's ill-mannered demeanor.

"Yes, lady." Ms. Blanchard quickly signed the papers for Sister Mary Anne after shoving the baby into the nun's arms. "If that is all, I would really wish to go now and return to my superiors." The governor's wife's assistant held her handbag a little tighter to her under arm, took one last look at the child that was just an hour ago the governor's child - but now belonged to the government - and said, "It's a pity, really - the way she came out like this; other than the little 'problem' on the one side of her head, she would've been just fine. But, all is well that ends well. If the two had decided to keep her, she would've been an embarrassment and mockery to the *both* of their families, indeed. But, on another note, good day, ma'am."

As Ms. Blanchard's ruthlessness almost bought a tear to
her eye, Sister Mary could barely find a way to say "Good day,"
as she watched the assistant disappear out of the double doors in
front of her. I'm sure the stunned and disturbed nun was quite
pleased to see the "mean, old bitty of an assistant" (as she later
described her) leave, at that very moment.

It was a colder winter night in this town, way back when
and Sister Mary was just about the only nun up that late, so
within moments, she found herself locking up the front doors of
this place and escorting little Delia to a room. She slowly walked
the long corridors with the beautiful baby girl of only one flaw in
her arms. Sister Mary Anne walked to a vacant room and just as
she began to unlock the door, a feeling of curiosity struck in her
mind. She barely opened the door when Delia kicked her little,
stubby legs, which reminded the curious nun that she had yet see
this mysterious child who had caused so much ruckus in the
governor's mansion and now, in this new institution.

Sister Mary Anne's curiosity and anxiousness grew as she
quickly reached the bed in the room she had chosen, without
disturbing Delia's position in her *own* arms too much. Once
Sister Mary had gotten the fragile, quiet baby unto the bed of the

room, she slowly began to peel the blanket atop Delia's face out of the way, as her eyes grew wider and wider in suspense. But, when she finally got the blanket back, her wide eyes grew into a warm smile that made Delia smile as well.

"So, this is what all of the fuss was about, was it? Nothing but an…" Sister Mary Anne paused and tilted her head to the side to get a better look at the, now, confused, yet still happy child, "…ear. Why, that's nothing to get all worked up about. I think it's quite charming or…cute, as you might say."

After this, Mary Anne simply took a gander at the child that had literally been abandoned by her parents "Such a sweet, precious child – one that should never be judged by a mere flaw that adds character and makes her beautifully unique. Here, we will never judge you by your minor flaws, darling, but, here at Heavenly Blessings, we shall only think of you as Delia Grennom, as you truly are a heavenly blessing." With that, the friendly nun completed little Delia's first night in her new home, after giving the little baby a bottle and rocking her to sleep. That, indeed, was the "ugly duckling's" first chapter in her new adventure and stay at this new place. I'm not sure if Delia knew it or not, but that was not the last or *only* adventure this little new born would have.

The next day was quite a day for the baby. As you might have already guessed, it had to start with the *whole* adoption home. That morning, just as every morning at Heavenly Blessings, was fairly hectic, but it was even more chaotic since they had just received a new arrival the night before. Every nun was racing and running to every room to open every window in the whole establishment; waking every well child from their beds; fixing the beds; preparing every eligible child's clothing; and finally getting every child ready for breakfast. As usual, there were quite a few nuns appointed to do each of the jobs as there were certainly far more children than nuns.

Delia was placed in Sister Mary Anne's quarters, so just as the sister finished with the other children she was appointed to assist, she was excited to be tending to Delia. She tried to stay content and ladylike, walking as fast as she could down the long hallways of the home just to get to Delia. The reason for the nun's frantically excited behavior was that Heavenly Blessing Adoption Home hadn't had or even seen a baby up for adoption for many, many years. But, because Sister Mary Anne was a nun - meaning she was not allowed to have a husband or children - and had always secretly wanted a baby, she was exceedingly thrilled to finally be able to take care of one. Although, just as a child that

172

is aware that they are not supposed to do wrong while they are doing so, Sister Mary Anne, at twenty-seven, knew better than any other nun at the home that one of the most important rules of Heavenly Blessings was to never get attached to any child there - even though the majority of them were there to stay. Therefore, she could not help having a feeling, in the back of her mind, that the other nuns probably wouldn't take to the newborn as easily as she did.

Approaching Delia's room, Sister Mary Anne thought of how her fellow sisters had previously acted with the few other babies that had been checked into the adoption home. They preached so much about how if it was against the rules for them to have children, why should they be teased with the infants; or how the babies were too much work compared to the other children. But, Sister Mary Anne tried her best to ignore those thoughts of what her fellow nuns would say, when she awoke Delia from her sleep, but quieted her with a pacifier she had found the night before. Just as she did this, Tina, one of the adoption home's most curious little girls, came creeping into Delia's room.

Fairly excited about the day, I suppose, Tina seemed to pop into the room, as she smiled and said "Sister Mary Anne!" The child startled the nun, leaving her with just enough time to cover the baby and turn around so that Tina wouldn't see her. "It's time to...what have you got there?"

Tina began to peer around Sister Mary in great curiosity. "What do I have?......oh here?......oh, nothing, Tina - nothing at all." Sister Mary thought herself to be a little silly to actually be *hiding* the infant at first, but she soon came to her senses, realizing she *was* the adult in the situation and shouldn't have to *hide* anything from a little four year old. "But, the better question is, Tina, what are you doing in this room? You know the other sisters would have my neck if they noticed that you weren't at breakfast this instant, but in a room with me...snooping." Sister Mary Anne made a quick gesture to get Tina out of the room by basically shoving her out the door.

"But Sister Mary Anne...." Tina began but was interrupted by the sister's strict tone.

"No, excuses, Tina; I want you to go to breakfast, this instant. Run along now." Sister Mary watched Tina walk all the way down the hallway, the whole time thinking of Delia still trapped under her cover. And just as soon as the girl disappeared, Sister Mary, to this day, still couldn't believe that she dashed back into the room so fast her skirt almost flew up past her knees. She then took Delia from under the cover, swept her up into a thicker blanket (to make her look like a bundle of sheets) - gazing at her little smile - and finally made her way to the nun's office.

In a sense, Sister Mary Anne began to fear what the other nuns would think of her for being the one to present the baby to them, but on another note, she had already said her morning prayer and had a feeling that everything would be all right. Still, she found herself dashing through every hallway of the home just as fast as her long, thin legs could take her, for she knew she didn't have long before it was time to start breakfast in the cafeteria. The sister had been walking for some time with her head down to reach her destination when she finally arrived at the front doors of the cafeteria. The cafeteria was the pathway to the Nun's Quarters, the special meeting place of all nuns in the establishment.

Mary almost feared having to walk in front of all the children in the cafeteria. She stood in front of the double doors with one hand on the handle and one under Delia, her own heart beat beginning to rise. She said a short prayer to herself, once again, as she slowly opened the doors and began to slowly stride across the room. She could see Tina sitting at a table nearest her as she made her way to the separate set of doors on the other side of the room and the children began to whisper and wonder about just what this nervous nun had bundled in her arms. The sister knew the children shouldn't be half of her worries, compared to the trouble she had lying ahead of her, behind the farthest cafeteria wall, in the Nun's Quarters.

"Good morning, sisters." Sister Mary Anne barely found the strength to whisper, stealthily emerging into the Nun's Quarters.

All the nuns happened to be arranged in their seats, talking amongst each other or more so shouting in disappointment. They were all convened in the room for their usual morning meeting, but Sister Mary Anne happened to be the only one that wasn't present.

One of the nuns was not the happiest to see her fellow sister; she was the disenchanted abbess, if you will. "*Good morning, sisters?*" Disgusted, she rose to her feet and almost stormed towards Sister Mary Anne, while the other nuns scornfully watched. Sister Mary Anne could only attempt to stand her ground; although, her hair was frayed from practically running down the hallway and her face was rather surprised-looking and fearful, in the same moment. "Sister Mary Anne, are we not supposed to convene here after preparing the children for breakfast, one hour before we are usually scheduled to convene, when there are new arrivals? God forgive me, but there is really no reason for this, sister...especially not..." the sister finished in a questioning and baffled tone, "...*to do laundry?*"

Sister Patrice continued her look of disappointment towards Sister Mary, as she had no regard to the fact that the bewildered nun was desperately trying to say something. "It is not even the time for laundry, Sister Mary. I cannot believe you would do this after all that we have put into this program...."

"But, Sister..." Mary Anne tried to interrupt but clearly wasn't going to get a single word in, as Sister Patrice continued her relentless chastising.

"Don't even bother to explain, Mary Anne; this is an utter disappointment to the whole staff and..." Sister Patrice's speech seemed to go on and on until Sister Mary Anne finally interrupted and blurted out, "Sisters, with all due respect, this is not laundry! And I was, by no means, late for no reason…"

The interrupting seemed to be a trend that day, as Sister Patrice cut in once again, "Then, *what is it, Mary?*"

"*It* is a baby." Sister Mary Anne pulled the bundled sheets from little Delia's face, as the whole congregation stepped back aghast and the clueless baby just smiled and made a fragile little sound.

Sister Patrice joined the majority of the congregation, saying "*My goodness!*" as she stepped forward, wide-eyed at the baby girl in Sister Mary's arms. She could hardly find the words, so the more enlightened nun went on. "Her name is Delia Lucille Grennom and she was delivered to us last night by the parents' assistant, herself."

Sister Patrice's hand stayed perched over her mouth, as she and the rest of the nuns were still amazed by the whole situation "The cause of arrival…"

Sister Mary took a quick look at the happy child's ear and looked at her fellow sister's eyes. "As unfortunate and vain as it is, I believe you can tell just what that is, Patrice."

Patrice's only response was a quick glance at Delia's ear and a dropped jaw for what seemed to be minutes...

That morning was very hectic, but after all of the morning chores, the children's lessons, and lunch, the chaos began to calm down a bit as Sister Mary thought. When she passed one of the open doors of a room in the main corridor, she soon discovered that there was more trouble to come.

"Oh, Sister Diane! Saying the child is odd-looking is saying the least and with a name like Delia, I can't imagine her getting too far," one of the two nuns in the room said as Sister Mary tried to fight her urge to eavesdrop on the conversation, which quickly overpowered her.

"Well, I'm just surprised Patrice actually let the thing stay here. There hasn't been a baby in Heavenly Blessings in years, Sara." The pudgier nun paused as if she had to think for a second, "Ah, well, she is probably counting on the fact that that Mary Anne is bound to get attached to the infant just like all the other infants. After all, do you think it was a coincidence she was the one to present the baby to us all? I certainly do not!"

At this point, Sister Mary Anne was surely prepared to barge into the room steamed and upset, but she kept her poise and lady-like manner as she demurely eased into the room with total self-control. "Hope I'm not interrupting anything, sisters, but I couldn't help but to overhear your conversation from the hall." Sister Mary was amused when both of the nuns jump at her arrival as they both said, "Sister Mary" in an appalled manner; Mary Anne couldn't care any less at the moment.

"Are you surprised I listened in, ladies, or would you have rather it been Sister Patrice?" Sister Mary seemed as stern and serious as a fever during cold and flu season, while her dark brown eyes seemed to pierce the two sisters, staring in some discomfort.

"You're the one who should be ashamed of yourself –
eavesdropping on our conversation..." Sister Diane, the pudgier
and older nun, began but was quickly interrupted by Sister Mary.

"Oh, please, sister! God knows the both of you were wrong
for the things you said, regardless and I don't mean to bother, but
there are few things I would like to say. Now, Delia is just as
good as any other child ever placed here at Heavenly Blessings,
despite the little issue on the side of her head, which should not
be anything of a problem, in the first place. Our job here is to
take care of every child *and* infant placed under our care and if
you all do not want the *burden* of the child, well..."Sister Mary
increased the severity in her voice as she stepped forward "...by
God's word, I'd be happy to do the rightful deed because as we
*all* know, whether we choose to admit to it or not, she deserves it.
With that, I bid you good day, sisters."

After those meaningful words, there was not another word
shared between the two nuns because there should not have been
anything spiteful to say in the first place. I am also pleased to tell
you that that was just about the last time Sister Mary Anne ever
had to deal with the rude comments about Delia Lucille...at least
not as much. The next few days, or weeks for that matter, instead

of disagreeing with the fact that little Delia was actually there the
nuns convened to organize their schedule to fit the baby into it,
as little Miss Grennom was the only baby in the entire home.
Although the nun's attitudes *improved*, I did not say that they
were perfect. Therefore, Sister Mary Anne did tend to receive the
most work for the infant since the other nuns miraculously
started to *volunteer* to take care of the rest of her block of
children, as long as she promised to *"tend* to...*her"* - a choice of
words Mary Anne was starting to hear more and more from the
nuns of Heavenly Blessings. I should suppose that it is a
wonderful thing that Mary Anne is the benevolent and loving
person she is or that she has the love for babies (and all children,
for that matter) that she has, because she took very kindly to the
fact that the other nuns were being as fickle and ultimately
selfish as they were being; it gave her more time with the
precious child that she knew hardly anything about.


The kindhearted nun enjoyed sneaking away during lunch
with the other children to be with the little baby; she enjoyed
feeding the baby right before the other children went to dinner in
the evenings; she adored washing Delia before bed and cradling
the child to help her fall asleep at night. Sister Mary Anne didn't
mind the fact that the child was a bit work or the fact that,
whether she realized it or not, she unknowingly assumed the role
of Delia's new...mother. Although, unwisely, I do believe there

was a fairly large part of the nun that wanted to be just that to little Delia.

Mary Anne watched the child grow to be a month old before she realized the longevity of the task ahead of her. But, once again, I do believe she would soon find out, for some of the other children in the home got their first look at the baby, one day, when she was scheduled to see the adoption home's nurse.

Tina, the little mischievous girl presented to you previously, *just happened* to be following Mary Anne's every step on her way to the nurse's office, but this particular day she just would not cease to annoy Sister Mary.

"Sister Mary, Sister Mary." Tina followed alongside the troubled nun, who was already sighing.

"Yes, Christina," Sister Mary firmly answered.

"Are you doing laundry, sister? What are you doing? I want to know." Tina reached her hand up and began to peel back the blanket, covering Delia's face.

"Christina Renee Billups, you had better cease this act of disobedience, this instant!" Sister Mary howled, snatching the cover back over Delia's face. Delia only babbled, almost loud enough for Tina to hear.

"Oh, please, please, Sister Mary." Tina grabbed at the blanket once again, only this time it happened to fall completely off of Delia's whole body.

All Tina could do was gasp, right before the *entire* hallway full of children. The rage in Sister Mary's eyes was quickly dispersed amongst all of the children present, for Tina's sake. "What in God's name do all of you find to be so amusing?" The agitated nun turned to face the rest of the children, still keeping an eye on Tina as she went on. "Is it the fact that she is a little different from the rest of you or is it just the plain fact that she is an infant, something I would have a fairly hard time believing!"

Afraid to answer after all she had caused, Tina raised her quivering little hand and stuttered, "M-m-m-maybe because the baby has....a...a...a... big ear, Sister Mary Anne."

"I thought so!" Sister Mary Anne started as her tone became even more overbearing. She would not normally raise her voice to anyone, but she was doing so, quite often, lately "Well, I will certainly tell you, Christina Renee'-just because this child is a little different from you does not make her any less important." She then turned to the whole hallway and said loud enough for them all to hear, "And to all of you - the entire congregation of children in this home - whether you all like it or not, you are going to have to accept the fact that little Delia is here and make an effort to ignore this little 'problem' you all seem to think she has. God made us all equally and beautifully different in our own ways and it's time that everyone would acknowledge that."

After the speech, Mary Anne briskly disappeared to the nurse's office to avoid any more confusion, leaving Tina and all of the other children in the hallway in awe. But, what she did not know was that Sister Patrice had heard the speech also – every word...

Little Delia's visit to the nurse's office was a brisk one. Fortunately, the nurse was not as absurdly callous as everyone else was. Delia was quickly examined and Sister Mary was told things she knew all too well already. After the visit, Sister Mary put Delia down for a nap and finished off the rest of her day, seeming to juggle the baby and her usual chores on one shoulder. But, soon it was all of no concern to Sister Mary, as she sat rocking the little baby girl in a chair she had found in one of the store rooms of the orphanage. She looked into her big, twinkling, brown eyes and rubbed her little ear and only thought of how precious the little infant was and how much life was going to have in store for her. Although, I feel terribly inclined to admit that it was still very difficult for the poor woman not to trouble herself with the thought of how everyone else was treating the baby girl, as she still could not understand how selfish and coarse they were behaving.

"Oh, my precious little Lucy," Sister Mary said to Delia Lucille (or Lucy, as she had begun to call her), while she had peacefully begun to fall asleep. "You, my dear, are such a precious child with so much to offer...things to offer that everyone seems to be unable to see. But, you are special, my dear...Oh so special." Yet again, Lucy was not the only one to hear these words as she drifted off to her pleasant dreams, because Sister Patrice stood at the crack of the door, listening.

Despite the moment above, I must say that time only seemed to fly by in Heavenly Blessings, as time has a knack for doing things of the sort. Just as the seasons passed and every other child increased in age in the home, so did little Delia grow older. Time passed on, the home was run as it usually was, and before anyone could realize it, six years had passed by. The home had become a little more sensitive to having Delia around, but I do believe that it is such a shame that even after six years of her being there, they were not entirely friendly towards her. The most shame seems to come from the fact that it was no longer because of her age, but because of her flaw. The big ear had only appeared to be even more prominent as she aged; the poor dear was such a tiny and fragile young girl and anything different could have seemed enormous on her. But, as you may also already known, Sister Mary Anne never gave up the fight for the precious little one.

After six years and the small sixth birthday she secretly threw for Delia (against the rules of the home), the diligent nun had still continued to care for Delia as her own child, in spite of the comments she would still hear, occasionally, from other nuns - after all, she was still the main caretaker of the child. In the six years that had passed, nothing had drastically changed. Although, more nuns were used to Delia, they still did not accept her for her appearance, but the other children were the worst part of the entire ordeal. Delia had grown to be a petite young girl with long, deep brown hair and big beautiful eyes to match. She had the cutest little button nose, cheeks that fogged with candy apple red whenever she was bashful and she spoke in the tiniest, delicate tone of voice imaginable. She always carried herself as the little lady she was, but her peers could only seem to care about the only thing that made her different - the only thing that seemed to radically separate her from the rest of them: her ear. They had even begun to refer to her by the horrid nick name of "Ugly Duckling," which caused Delia to instantly burst into tears.

Such a sweet little one Delia developed into, because the hurtful things her peers may have said about her seemed to never really affect who she was as a person. This may have had something to do with the fact that Mary Anne tried to keep her secluded from the rest of the group as much as she could, even though her efforts were scrutinized by Sister Patrice and the other nuns, as were many of the things Sister Mary tried to do for the little girl. They did not agree with Sister Mary's acts of "babysitting Delia every chance she could"; they felt she should "fend for herself" and that she should be "left to socialize with the other children" or "hang to dry" as Sister Mary often phrased it. Patrice even seemed to scold Sister Mary about calling the little girl Lucy from time to time, only because she knew the real reason behind it; otherwise, she would not have been alarmed by the nick name in the least bit. But, despite all of this ruckus and drama, Delia still developed into a mature and beautiful little girl and over the few years she had been raised by Sister Mary, she had developed the talent of the singing. She loved to bless the nun with her little tunes occasionally, and she even enjoyed singing by herself. Unfortunately, she did not know that it was this talent that could also cause her just a bit of trouble...

I seem to remember a particular instance that little Lucy was in the play room of the orphanage, amongst the other children. She mainly enjoyed playing with dolls on her own, but today she happened to be sitting in a window far from anyone else, enjoying the weather of the colder spring day. The pretty little one was not merely sitting there, but she was once again lost in her own world of song; on this particular day, she had chosen a song of spring and joy. She was singing so delightfully that one may have forgotten that she was only a little girl, whose beauty shown incredibly through the plain clothes of Heavenly

189

Blessing's uniform. Sadly, as striking as the sound of her voice
was, it did not take but a single act of malevolence to shatter the
moment of splendor. A poke on her little fragile shoulder did just
that.


"Hey, ugly duckling, could you be quiet? We're trying to
play, but all we can hear is your ugly voice!" a little boy around
Delia's age shouted, as his friends stood behind him. He was a
usual bully of Delia's, but the poor girl did not even know his
name.


She only looked at him with her piercing antique chestnut
eyes, and without a single word, began to walk away. But before
she could hardly take a few steps, the boy started again "Ugly
duckling! You ugly little duckling! Big-eared duckling! You ugly
duckling!" the boy still chanted, while his friends joined in.


Delia tried to keep herself together but the tears just began
to flow, as she shouted, "Leave me alone!" Delia's cry caught the
attention of the nun that was watching over the children, but by
the time she could reach the poor girl, the other children had
already surrounded her, continuing their horrible chant.

"Ugly duckling! Ugly little duckling!" was all Delia could hear, aside from the shouting of the younger nun for them to stop, as she covered her ears and tears were still cascading to the floor. Then suddenly, she felt two arms around her and she was being pulled out of the circle.

Right then a voice took over that seemed much louder than it really was. "Stop this, this instant!" The rage in the woman's tone of voice would have led one to believe that she was naturally a firm person, but she really was not – not in the least. "Go away! All of you! Go back to what you were doing, right now!" Delia was in the arms of the one person that seemed to care for her – the one person that always seemed to protect her, no matter what: Sister Mary Anne. She stood a little taller than she was, six years before - maybe just a couple inches – but her height still complemented her more mature and lengthier frame. Her hair fell further down her back in even more of a richer brown than it was before and her eyes got sharper, yet brighter with her age. Now, she seemed to tower above the other children, as they scurried about their ways and the younger nun watched, scared to say anything. Mary Anne only glanced at her, before she left the room with Delia on her hip.

"Are you all right, darling?" Sister Mary looked softly into Delia's eyes, as the child still clung to her and her tears began to dry.

"I will be fine, Sister Mary," Delia announced. She was perched atop Sister Mary's hip, but the little lady was determined to regain her composure – that was always a part of her charm.

Sister Mary looked her over once again, like a mother to her own child, still afraid to let her down, but she knew she had to. "All right, Lucy. Run along to your room and I will be there, shortly." A small smile came to Delia's face as her little feet touched the ground again and she nodded, before she skipped away.

Sister Mary had just begun to let a smile reach her own face, but the voice that sounded behind her *was* as pungent as it seemed and startled her all too quickly. "Mary Anne, I need to see you in the Nun's Quarters." Sister Mary slowly turned to see Sister Patrice glaring at her in almost pure disgust. Her hair was grayer and she mostly wore it pulled back, which exposed her very serious eyes and face that had developed more lines over the years and only added to her grave demeanor. Sister Mary could

192

sense the fact that she was in trouble as Sister Patrice walked right by her - her arms folded in front, a stern look on her older face.

"You know, Mary Anne, I have been meaning to share what I am about to share with you for quite some time now, but I did not know exactly how to say it." Sister Patrice was pacing the pews of the Nun's Quarters, as Mary Anne's stature seemed to be dwindling before her own eyes; she felt like the children she had scolded not too long before that moment. "I wish there were a better way to put this, but you know as well as anyone else that I have never been one to evade the truth, no matter how gruesome it may seem. On another note, I have always known you to be one that sticks to her convictions and does what she feels is right, regardless of the circumstances; although, I also know that very same attitude could cause a bit of trouble, from time to time..."

"Excuse me for interrupting, Sister, but what exactly are you getting at?" Sister Mary's eyes were frozen on the abbess, but she was not completely dumbfounded. She knew where the situation was going; she just did not approve of it.

Suddenly Patrice's pacing came to a halt right in front of Mary Anne, as she continued, "You have got to stop the way you treat Delia; your actions have been going on for too long now and they certainly need to stop."

Sister Patrice's face was as harsh as can be, but Mary Anne's disgust at what she had just said was too strong to merely sit there. "With all due respect, Sister, I too believe some things have certainly been going on for too long in this home – things that I, too, have been trying not to mention for the sake of the children and this establishment, as well..." Sister Patrice knew exactly what she was speaking of, but she ignored those truths and stuck to her judgments.

The older nun stepped closer to the younger and went on, "I do not know exactly what you are speaking of, Mary, but the facts of the matter remain as such: you are spoiling the child and all are beginning to notice." Patrice was practically breathing on Sister Mary's nose as she said, "It must stop"

Mary could restrain herself no longer, as the anger in her heart only began to increase more and more. She stood to her feet and did something she had never before conjured up in her mind to do... "I believe it is only the contraire, Patrice." The other sister was becoming extremely frustrated herself, but she was still surprised by Mary Anne's actions, as she shouted, "Mary Anne..."

Unfortunately, her efforts were to no avail; the younger nun was determined to say exactly what she had been yearning to say to this woman for quite some time. All she could think of was how wrong they treated the poor little girl she had almost single-handedly raised for years all because of their selfishness and their prejudices and their border-line malice toward her. "I have heard enough of your foolishness and your ignorance, just as well as everyone else's! I cannot even believe that you have allowed yourself to be bamboozled by these evil ways! You actually believe what you are saying to be true, Sister! How can you be this way! She is a child, who needs care and attention, just as any other child in this home..."

"Now, wait just one moment. No one is telling you to abandon her..."

"But that is exactly the case! I have raised her on my own for the past six years – it started off as extra shifts and a little here, accompanied by a little there and now, it is as if I am the only one who does the work, the only one who cares!" Patrice

195

tried to interrupt once again, but Mary Anne was in no position to let her carry on, as her height suddenly seemed to soar over the older nun and she put her back in her place. "Listen to me when I say that anything that I could possibly do to "*spoil*" that child, as you say, is nothing but what you all have been depriving her of ever since we took her in, six years ago! That poor baby has been tormented and scrutinized ever since her birth and it seems to me that you are trying to pacify the possible jealousy and imprudence of the other nuns and children in this home by getting me to ignore the child...."

"Mary Anne, you have no idea what you are speaking of! You are out of your place and I am going to have to ask you to retire to your quarters for the remainder of the day."

"I will leave, Sister Patrice, but you just make sure you remember this, as you sleep tonight." Sister Mary Anne's tone elevated to one to be respected, as she raised her finger to Patrice and went on with clenched teeth and an anger in her tone that I am sure no one had ever known she could possess. "For the things we do not speak out against, today, we will suffer for tomorrow and if we do not, once in our short and momentary lives, dare to push against the norm and remain steadfast against the thoughts and ignorance of others, I shall say that we will only be immobile in a state of ignorance of our own..."

Mary Anne watched as Sister Patrice's face was as still and solemn as an innocent child, who could do nothing but be intrigued, yet stunned by the words she was hearing, "Now, one day that child will be a woman and I am sure that she will not wish to look back on the dreary and unfair childhood she had because of the negative chauvinism of those that were supposed to care for and love her." Mary Anne took a step back and looked directly into the eyes of her successor. "And if anything else, that child will only have the capacity to despise the one woman who had the most control over her life, but chose to use it to take away the one person who did care for and love her, and if she shall, so help you God..."

With that, Sister Mary Anne's petite and lengthy figure scurried off towards the door of the massive space of the Nun's Quarters, but before she could exit the room, Patrice added one last remark. "You are not her mother, Mary Anne!" Mary Anne stopped in her tracks, as the words seemed to stop her heart and rob the oxygen from her lungs. She turned halfway towards Patrice... "And you never will be!" Mary Anne stood by the door, half-turned away in shock, as she listened to what was just said to her, right before she slammed the double doors of the room and disappeared into the cafeteria.

Patrice turned her cheek in the other direction as she let Mary Anne slip away to her own thoughts, but I am afraid that neither that little notion nor anything she could possibly do, would ever be enough to ignore the words the younger woman had just said...

Her feet seemed to pound into the floor, as Mary stormed through the hallways and called much attention to herself after leaving Patrice. As enraged and livid as she was, Mary Anne felt she would never get what Patrice had said or how all the other nuns and even the children treated poor little Delia, out of her mind. She just could not understand how they could treat the child that way, after all she had been through or for all that she was as a person. She refused to understand and she felt she would never try.

"Sister Mary, Sister Mary," Tina said, interrupting her favorite nun's thoughts, with her usual pestering behavior and a very unwanted jovial smile.

Unfortunately for Tina, Sister Mary could barely constrain herself any longer. She was quickly making her way through the hallways and that seemed to be consuming all of her concern, at that very moment. "Tina, go to your room; this is not the time," were her only words, as she never stopped walking just as briskly as she had been.

"But, Sister Mary, there's something I want to show you..." Tina was waving that day's paper in her hand, trying to get Mary Anne's divided attention.

"Tina!" Mary suddenly stopped with a look in her eyes that had only been there but a few times before; she didn't even notice that Sister Sara and Sister Diane were staring at her, the entire time. "I have just told you that this is not the time for any type of conversation!" Little ten-year-old Tina tried to interrupt again, but failed horribly. "Now, unless it is an emergency of some kind, I want you to run along and wait until later! That is it!"

Little Tina's upper lip began to quiver, as she slowly lifted the newspaper to Sister Mary's hand. "I j-j-j-just wanted to tell my favorite sister that I read the newspaper, today, for the first time..." The child was an extremely late reader because of her dyslexia, and she had finally reached the reading level of complex literature such as the *London Times*.

Ashamed and embarrassed, Sister Mary took the newspaper from the poor girl, but she stormed off with tears streaming down her face, before she could even say a word. Troubled as she was, she could only yell "Tina, please come back! Tina..." as the little one disappeared around the corner. Mary Anne finally saw the piercing set of eyes of the other two nuns upon her, as she hung her head in shame. Disappointed, she scurried off to her own room.

When Sister Mary finally arrived at her place of study, she closed the door behind her and fell into the chair nearest the door, letting the newspaper plummet into her lap. Her tears quickly followed behind it; she had finally reached her limit. She wept and thought for hours about what Patrice had said, what Delia had to experience, and her own personal struggles. She had no idea of what she was to do or who she was to turn to; all she had was this situation and this child and all the troubles that came along with both of the happenings. Mary Anne knew Patrice had been right on one respect; she was not fulfilling all of her duties to all of the children in the home. She *did* allow herself to give Delia far more attention than anyone else, even if it was for good reasons – reasons Patrice seemed not to understand. Just as she began to cry to God for help, she finally looked at the newspaper Tina had given her and she began to feel horrible about how she had treated the poor girl; it was the first newspaper she had ever read and she wanted to share it with her, her favorite nun.....The article was in *The London Times*...."Governor Grennom and Wife Said to Have Had Newborn..".

Even through the blur of her vision from her tears, this article, in particular, caught the attention of Mary Anne, as she collected herself enough to read on: *Recently, reporters have found that the new child of the governor and his wife is, despite what the media had been swayed to believe, not their first child, but their second. We have no further information about the "missing," first child of the family*....Mary Anne needed to read no more; the last name Grennom had already initiated many thoughts in her mind, as she thought back to the very first night Delia was admitted to the home. She almost jumped out of her seat in amazement, as she gazed at the picture of the governor, his wife, and 'newborn'. She remembered the assistant who brought little Delia in and what she said that made her hate her, almost immediately, "*It* is....- well, I'll keep their names confidential for the sake of their reputation – but whose *it* is should be of no concern, lady. She was just born today and they don't want her. I can't say I blame them, because if you were to have one good look at her head, you would know for yourself the reason that is as clear as day itself."


It was all too clear to her now: Delia was the governor's child and they had given her up for the same reason that no one wanted anything to do with her in the orphanage. They had intentionally abandoned her for six years – essentially all her life - because of one little flaw. She wept about this for some time, as well, but she could not stand it any longer and decided to go and see Delia – she had to. Mary Anne gathered herself immediately and silently scurried through the hallways; it was well after eight 'o'clock at night and everyone was supposed to be sleeping. Her hair was frazzled and her cheeks were still damp from her tears, but she just had to see the poor child after what she had most recently read.


Upon arriving at little Lucy's room, Mary Anne silently cracked open the door and slipped inside. There she was – that small, fragile, precious person she had come to know so well. Delia lay fast asleep under her covers. Apparently someone had actually fed and put her to sleep, something that took Mary Anne by great surprise. But, that was of no concern to her now as she sat beside this precious child, who was so oblivious to everything that was happening and remained so happy and beautiful through it all. Mary Anne had just begun to stroke her face when the little lady awoke.

"Sister Mary, what are you doing in here? I've missed you all day." Lucy's little voice was music to Sister Mary's ears and the little child suddenly sat up in bed and hugged her dearly.

This almost brought tears to her eyes as she hugged Delia tighter. "My precious child of God, if only you knew..." was all Mary Anne could say, because she knew she could not yet tell the child who her parents were.

Suddenly Delia pulled away from Mary Anne to look directly into her eyes. "Sister Mary, today in Bible study, we talked of Adam and Eve and Sister Diane was talking about Eve and her family. Sister Diane said that a mother is someone who cares for, loves, and protects her children. I wanted to ask you something about that..."

"Yes, darling, anything in the world." Mary Anne looked intently into the eyes of this sweet child, having no idea what question would come.

Delia batted her pretty little eyes and looked just as innocent as ever. "Does that mean you're my mother?"

Mary Anne was simply taken aback by the words Lucy had just spoken. She instantly thought of the words Patrice had spoken to her only moments before. She thought of all the moments she had spent with the child; she thought of the newspaper article and all Delia had been through and all that she felt and how much she cared for her and how much she so unconditionally loved her.

"I..." Mary Anne held her tears back for as long as she could, but they obstinately began to flow. "I am afraid we will have to continue this conversation another night, Delia." It was barely a whisper, as she quickly wiped away her tears.

"But..." Delia tried to continue, but Mary Anne's mind was all made up.

"Now, now, you heard what I said, Lucy. It is time for you to go back to sleep." Delia said not another word as Mary Anne quickly tucked her under her covers, kissed her on her cheek, and got out of the room as quickly as possible.

All Sister Mary could think of was how attached she really was to this child and how she had irresponsibly let Lucy begin to believe that she was her mother. But, if Mary Anne was not, who was? Her parents did not want her, the adoption home shunned her and she was the only one who cared. Mary Anne tried to make it to her room, but she could not and she burst out in tears right in the hallway and slumped down to the floor in distress.

The sun never shone through the windows of Heavenly Blessings the day after the instances mentioned above. It was a silent and rainy day in the adoption home, which meant everyone except the nuns was supposed to remain in their rooms, as silent as possible. Sister Mary seemed to be the first one awake, as she was staring out her window, out past the water collecting on the pane. It was but a few hours before it was time for the nuns to wake and get ready to serve the children breakfast. She had been up most of the night, tossing and turning, and in prayer about all that had happened in the last few days - but really, in the last six years. She had pondered and prayed over everything that had to do with her situation with sweet Delia, and God had finally brought her to a conclusion: she had only to acquire the courage to follow through with her ideals.

Soon Mary Anne was dressed and making her way out of her room. The only thing on her mind was Delia as she heard the pitter patter of the rain echoing throughout the halls. No one was up yet, when she had decided to check on Delia, before she made her last stop; the silence of the morning had started to discourage her, but Lucy's peaceful calmness reminded her of her cause. Mary Anne continued to Sister Patrice's quarters.

She closed her eyes hard, before she softly knocked on her door. It was only a quarter passed four o' clock in the morning when Mary Anne stood outside her superior's door, trembling from head to toe with the anxiety of it all. Just as her uneasiness reached its peak, the door of Sister Patrice's room suddenly opened and the older nun looked outside to see who it was.

"Mary Anne, what are you doing up at this hour?" Patrice barely whispered through the crack of the door, but before Mary Anne could answer, she opened the door wider. "Come in, child and sit."

Mary Anne slowly crept into the door and briskly closed it behind her. She immediately felt like a child who had done something wrong and was ready to confess it as she stared at Patrice from her seat on the side of her room.

"Well, what is it, Mary Anne?" Patrice's face was always so stern, but for the moment, it was not an easy task for her to conceal her uprising concern.

Sister Mary swallowed hard and softly began, her eyes hardly raised from the floor, "I've been up all night, thinking and praying..."

"About what?" Sister Patrice listened intently, her arms crossed and worry in her eyes.

"Have you seen yesterday's paper, Sister Patrice?" Mary Anne decided to get right to what she intended to speak of. Thinking of Delia, she could feel no more shame or fright.

"I did – a normal paper it was, I thought, dear; not enough to keep one up at four o'clock in the morning." Patrice crossed her legs and nonchalantly answered, as if she had no idea what Mary Anne was speaking of.

"*A normal paper*, Sister?" Mary Anne paused for a moment, almost in disbelief of the older nun, irritation suddenly flourishing within. "Coming here, I had no intentions of an argument, but you cannot say that the headline on the front page did not catch an ounce of your interest." Mary Anne's face grew serious with every word.

"Well, it didn't entirely, my dear." Patrice looked Mary Anne right in her eyes with no regret of her deceit.

"Sister..." Mary Anne stood up from her seat, "They're her parents!"

Sister Patrice stood up even quicker than Mary Anne did and stormed toward her. "You don't know that, Mary Anne! I would advise you to not only keep your voice down at this time of morning, but to reconsider mentioning that to anyone, because neither you nor I are sure of that fact, at all!" Patrice's eyes were as serious as a heart attack and the lines in her face seemed to show more with her anger. Mary Anne could not recall a time when the woman had been so infuriated.

She took a deep breath and focused on her point. "You're right, we don't know that, for sure. But one thing we do know is that she does not belong here."

"That's preposterous!" Patrice turned away, "She's an abandoned child just like any other child we are housing here."

"Is that we're doing here, Sister – *housing* children? Listen to yourself!"

"Listen to *your*self, Mary Anne!"

Patrice turned back around to face the young nun; suddenly, it was if she were begging her to understand. "You cannot save everyone, child; you knew that the moment you entered the convent and this home and..."

Tears began to well up in Mary Anne's eyes. She could find the strength to utter only one thing – it was all she had left, after fighting her cause for so long. "But I can save her."

"You don't know what you're saying, Mary Anne..." Patrice now spoke to her as a mother to her child – out of concern and with sincerity.

"I do know what I am saying and I *will* save her from this, because I *can*..." Mary Anne's eyes abruptly revealed the hurt she had experienced, watching Delia suffer as she had since her birth. The look on her face revealed to Patrice the undying love she had for the child – a love that was increasingly difficult to ignore.

Sister Patrice was almost in tears herself. "Do you know all that you would be giving up, Mary Anne? Do you know how long you've been here, child? This is your home!" Her eyes were like blazing furnaces, coals restless and unnerved. Mary Anne could not see that Patrice's heart was filling with hurt, as the time progressed and Patrice tried so desperately to hide her grief.

Sister Mary's tears were now flowing more than ever. "No! You're wrong...I don't belong here just as she doesn't and even if I did, I would be doing this for her. I love her with all my heart and she does not deserve the treatment she gets here. She has never deserved anything of this sort and I will not just throw my hands up and give up! I refuse...." The words escaped her mouth faster than she could have censored any of them, but after only a moment, she was thankful to have finally spoken her heart and revealed the truth.

Patrice turned her back to Mary Anne, at this point, as there was not much else she could do, she wept silently in the other direction and paused for a short while to collect her thoughts. "You are a strong young woman, my child, but you must know all that you are trying to do and all that you are giving up, before you go on, because if you do not, I shall fret that I will regret letting you go."

The deed was done as Mary Anne stepped toward Patrice, yearning to reach out to her. But, even though she only spoke to the back of her, she knew she was listening. "I now know what I want in life, Patrice, and I now know that that child is so special and she is being deprived of life here...."

"Then, go..." Sister Patrice interrupted, "Just go..."

Sister Patrice never turned around and Mary Anne never spoke another word while the tears fell incessantly from her eyes and she escaped from the room. She paused for only a moment by the door to take in all that had just happened. It was almost over, she thought as she inhaled deeply, before she immediately almost dashed to the room of little Delia.

Approaching the door, she heard a sweet, tiny little voice streaming throughout the hallways like an innocent spirit; the voice sounded all too familiar and so did the tune. Upon opening the door, accompanied by the sweet song now surrounding her ears, she saw this fragile little body dressed for the day, peering out of her window. "Rain rain go away, come again another day..." she repeatedly sang, before noticing that Mary Anne had entered the room. Sister Mary only stared in awe as a smile dawned on her face, revealing the relief in her heart and soul.

"Sister Mary, Sister Mary, did you see the rain?" the small child chanted, ambushing the slender nun by jumping into her arms.

Sister Mary carefully kneeled down to little Delia, her smile still extended from ear to ear and a love in her heart that she never had to ignore again. "I did, Lucy; I saw the rain..." Searching for the words to say, she looked right into Delia's eyes. "Darling, what would you say if I could take you away to a place where it would never rain again? Would you want to come with me?"

Delia nodded, as she too began to smile. "I would, Sister Mary Anne. I don't like it when it rains, especially not here."

The child didn't need to say anymore. Mary Anne grasped her in her arms and soon the two of them were walking out of the door of little Lucy's room. The hallways were crowded with nuns staring directly at them as soon as the door was opened. Mary

Anne saw Sister Diane and Sister Sara and all the other nuns that
had shunned her and mistreated her throughout the last six years.
Delia saw some of the children that had called her names and
judged her for the smallest portion of her that made her different.
Lastly, as the two of them headed to the front door hand-in-hand
and Sister Mary laid her headdress on the front counter, she
raised her forlorn, yet relieved eyes to see Sister Patrice staring,
before she seemed to disappear down the main corridor, a pain in
her heart that Sister Mary would never know of.

Mary Anne looked down at Delia, but it was no bother to
either of them while they made their final steps to the front door.
Sister Mary Anne was now just Mary Anne and "the ugly
duckling" was no more. Mary Anne cast open the tall, cathedral-
like doors of the adoption home and the sun emerged out of the
clouds and shone directly unto both of their faces. Standing there
in the light of the moment, Mary Anne knew she had done what
she needed to do. She did not know it at the time but she had
disappointed Sister Patrice many times throughout the course of
that situation, but to this day, Sister Patrice admits that she was
more proud of her then - glaring at her from across the lobby of
the front desk - than she had ever been of her, throughout her
*entire* stay at Heavenly Blessings.

Mary Anne grabbed *her child* up into her arms as the two of them made their way off the stoop of Number 114 Rockerdelle Lane and watched the rain wash away into the gutters and silently flow down the street...

"A man's errors are his portals of discovery"

James Joyce

# I Am Only a Man

On realization and so much more...

The cold wind that morning almost made my cheeks burn, as I looked down at her face, frozen in its place. A part of me was wishin' she would blink and sit up and hug me and kiss me the warm way she always used to, but she never did...Everybody else around me wasn't even there to me; it was like I was in a dream or somethin' and it was just me and my momma. I never thought I'd see the day that I would be standing over the only woman I thought I would ever love, as she lay lifeless in a casket. I was only seventeen and it wasn't fair; she was sup-posed to bury me, not the other way around. My whole body was caught in time while my eyes were glued on the beige dress covering her ivory skin and I had to stop myself from thinkin' of all the good she had done for me and every single thing she had taught me. She was the most beautiful, intelligent, and sweet woman in the world to me and now she was gone. It was funny, but I guess it was rain-in" for her, that day. I couldn't even move, thinking of it all and I didn't want them to close the casket but, as the rain slowly fell off of my nose unto hers, they did. All I could do was hold the picture of her long light brown hair, starry eyes, and beautiful face, too much like my own, in my head, all the way until me and my dad got back to our seats amongst the rest of the family, who suddenly reappeared. I held back every single tear I knew I wanted to cry, even though my eyes were startin' to glaze over and I was more hurt, in that moment, than I had ever been in my entire life.... I just silently hoped and prayed that I would never let that image escape me, as long as I lived....

The car ride home was pretty long; all I can remember is me and my dad riding back to the house, lookin' forward and not saying a word. My momma's face kept poppin' up in my head and I couldn't stop thinkin' about how much she meant to me or how life could be so cruel to me. I remember feelin' like half of me was gone. Even though I had my dad sittin' right next to me, half of me was six feet under the ground of the funeral home we had just left. That woman had given me half my greenish-brown eyes, my caramel skin, my light brown hair, my hands, my feet, my wisdom the little manners I did have - my everything...

"Son," my dad said. He always had a heavy voice, but he never knew just what to say. I knew he didn't now, especially not in that situation, for sure. I just looked at his dark brown skin and right into the black eyes of his always serious face, hoping he could say somethin' to make me feel like I wasn't gonna break down any time soon... "Never mind." That really disappointed me; I held back my tears, again, during the ride home...

At home, I couldn't wait to get to my room. Me and Dad still weren't say-in" a word, so that made it easier for me get upstairs. It wasn't that easy though, because all of a sudden I found myself waiting for my mom to come in behind us and start dinner or ask me: "Thomas, did you finish your homework? You got that big paper due tomorrow and you always procrastinate!" I smiled a little bit thinkin' of that, but I had to remember she wasn't comin' home, that time. I passed about five pictures of her on the stairwell goin' to my room. I hurried up there, ,,cause I thought I was reaching my breaking point.

"Thomas! Thomas! Thomas!" she was racin' around the house in a University of Florida sweatshirt and some jeans, calling me down from my room. The mail man had just come, so I guessed we got some good news.

"What's up, Mom?" I already had a smile on my face, just seeing her, so anything she had in that envelope would only make me feel better.
I made my way down the stairs and she had already torn open a letter. My dad wasn't home from work yet, so he wouldn't know what was goin' on, 'till later.

"*What's up! What's up!* Honey, U of F just sent you an acceptance letter. You have a full athletic scholarship for school!" I already knew I was gonna get in, but I liked to play around with her like that so I tried to look unconcerned.

"Oh that's *it?*" I went to get a banana in the dining room, trying to conceal my playful smile.

"*That's it!* Thomas, what are you talking about? This is big stuff!"
I laughed so hard it was ridiculous. "I'm just playin', Mom; I already knew about that. Coach told me yesterday; that letter is just a preliminary." Her face was priceless, while I pretended not to care and took a bite of my banana.

"Boy, you are such a snake!" she hit me with the envelope and started gigglin'.

Later on, I was turnin' in for the night, when she came in. "Baby, are you sleep?"     I sheepishly rolled over and squinted my eyes to see her at the door. "If I was, you just woke me up." I smiled at my joke.

"Hush, boy!" She made her way to my bed and sat down. "Listen, I want to talk to you about school." It seemed she always did her best lectures at night, when they were unexpected.

"What about?"

"Well, honey, you're getting older now and you've got to make older, more mature decisions."

219

"C'mom, Mom, haven't we had this talk before? I'm not having unprotected sex." I was always a joker, but I could tell it was really beginnin' to annoy her.

"Thomas, I'm serious." She turned on the light by my bed and looked right into my eyes. "Neither me nor your father will be around forever to help you and guide you to turn you into the man that we both know you can be. You will be *eighteen years old* soon and it is your responsibility to make responsible choices and be a responsible adult; do you understand me?"

"I know, Momma." I looked at her a while, and then she hugged me real tight and kissed me on the cheek.

"Sleep on it and promise me you'll make good decisions, Thomas." Her blue eyes were so serious, right then, as I looked into them for longer. I could tell by the look in her eyes that there might have been more behind her words; I'll never forget it.

"I will, Momma. I will."

I didn't wanna come back, but I had to. The shower was freezin' before I realized I was lost in a flashback. I didn't turn the knob to hot because I wasn't really there. I was back in a time when my mother was alive and well, which was only weeks before. It's funny, because she died of a heart attack – Karen Alice Barnett, the healthiest woman I knew, died of a heart attack at thirty-eight. It took both me and my dad by surprise. She was only twenty years older than me. It happened at work one day, but I had a feeling she already knew she had heart problems. It occurred to me that night she talked to me about "responsibility." She said, "Neither me nor your father will be around forever to help you..." so I think she knew she had heart problems for a while, actually. That made me really angry 'cause she should have told me. Me and Dad knew she never liked people to feel sorry for her, but right then in the shower, she left me to only feel sorry for myself. My eyes started to glaze over again, but it was harder to hold the tears back that time.

My dad always told me that real men don't cry - that they just get angry and even - but I could never get even with God and my anger faded when I realized that I would never see the one woman I had the most respect for, whom I had always admired and cherished, again. I turned the shower on hot and sobbed like a baby. I didn't want my dad to hear, so I turned the knob to high and just let the water pour over me to hide the tears streamin' down my face. The only woman I thought I'd ever love was gone forever.

Me and Danielle had been on and off for a while and we couldn't decide whether or not we wanted to take a break. We were both going off to college by the end of the summer, but I couldn't even think of that when I was walking her to class the next day. It was so quiet between us, you could hear a pin drop and she didn't even bother asking what was wrong; she knew what was up. Me and my dad still hadn't said much to each other, so you know I definitely had hardly anything to say to her, either.

"I guess I'll see you later, baby." When she said that, I looked into the same light brown eyes I had known for that past year we'd been dating, before I answered. She looked real concerned but there was nothing I could do. "Baby, everything is going to be okay. You'll be-"

"I'll see you later, okay?" I didn't want to talk about it. I didn't even kiss her goodbye. I just walked down the hall to my Calculus class.

Danielle Griffin was one of the prettiest girls in school. She wasn't a cheerleader like you might have guessed but aside from her hazel eyes and beautiful body, it was (surprisingly) her personality that I loved *almost* more than anything. She was always there for me and took anything I dished out, including my wandering eyes. I was comfortable with her and she made me happy, but even she couldn't fix what had just happened that past weekend – not at all.

"He's a man, Karie. Ain't nothin' wrong with keeping his options open." My Dad always took my side on stuff like girls, but it annoyed the hell out of my momma.

"Larry, I can't believe you just said that. This boy asks our advice and this is what you tell him?" Dad started to say somethin', but Mom cut 'em off; I had to hold in my laughter. "Listen, Son, if you really care about this girl, you won't see other girls behind her back."

"But, Mom..." I tried to tell her we were on a break in our relationship.

"There are no objections to that, Thomas. You have her thinking you care about her and that she is the only girl you want right now. I did not raise you to be a heartbreaker, Thomas. I raised you to be a respectable, loyal young man."

"Barnett! What'chu doin', man? What's up" I completely forgot I was at football practice. I was supposed to be strappin' up, but instead I was lost in the past. This time, it was later in the year before and my mom was talking to me about Danielle. Big Ben, our quarterback, was hoverin' over me with a confused face.

223

"Oh, uh...nothin', man; let's go." I jumped up to get on the field. I didn't want anybody to see me down, especially not my team members.

I was heading towards the door, when Ben caught me by the shoulder, "Hey, man, we all know about your mom. I know you were really close, so if you ever need to get anything off your chest..."

"Naw, I'm all right." I hurried out the door and headed to practice.

Classes seemed to go by slow that day, probably because I was so quiet. I hadn't seen my girl since that morning and by the time I texted her, I was already at home. I was expectin' my dad to be at work, but he was sitting at the dining room table, lookin' all deep in thought.

He looked at me as soon as I got in the door and I froze like a deer in the headlights; I didn't know what to think. "Come sit with me, Son."

I remember starting to say, "I got a lot of homework" or "I gotta get ready for this party," but I didn't. I was curious. I just wanted to know what he was gonna say, even if it *was* awkward.

224

"How was your day?" He looked me right in the eyes, but I couldn't help looking down a little. Even though he was beatin' around the bush, it was the first time we really talked since the funeral. I barely said "fine," when he went on.

"Listen, Son." I could tell he was searching for the words, "I know this is hard for you and it's hard for me, too."

"Dad, we don't have to do this." It was easier for me to avoid the situation and all that came with it, if that was even possible.

"I want to, Thomas. It's the only way the two of us can move on with our lives." Those words struck me all too hard; instantly, I was too angry to be timid.

"How are we supposed to do that, Dad – just forget her?" I knew he didn't mean any harm, but still.

"That's not what I mean."

"Then what do you mean, Dad?"

"I mean, she's gone, boy, and she's not comin' back!" He stood up all of a sudden and was towering over me. I couldn't help but to feel a small bolt of fear shoot up my spine. "The faster we realize that, the faster we can deal with it and live the lives she would've wanted us to!"

*Damn.* I couldn't really say anything to that, 'cause I knew he was right. His words struck me like a slap in the face and it was kinda hard for me to accept it all so fast. It was all just so difficult – difficult to accept the fact that my mother was dead, difficult not to cry, difficult to live without her and not really be able to share my feelings with my father for fear of what this other man would think of my weakness.

"I'm here going through the same thing, Son. I'm here and that's all I can do." He walked out of the dining room then, but to this day only God knows I didn't want him to go.

"Dad," I said. He stopped as I stood up, but he didn't turn around at first. "I miss her." The words seemed to sneak out of my mouth, but I didn't have to say anything else. By the time I could say the last word, he had already run to me and grabbed me into a hug – a real tight hug – and he just held me in the silence.

I could feel my eyes glaze over again – I guess I really couldn't help it those days. It made me feel weak to even want to cry, though. "Don't do that, Son." Suddenly my dad pulled me away and looked at me. "Don't do that. Tears are not gonna bring her back, Thomas." I hadn't even started to cry, but maybe he sensed it. "We only have men in this house from now on; you hear me?"

It took a minute to sink in, because the tears sometimes helped me cope with the issue but I knew that it wasn't good for a man to cry. I just nodded in answer to 'em and let it go.

It took me a lil while to recuperate from that conversation, but I had to "strap back up" (my coach used to say that all the time), be a man, and realize what's done is done, no matter how much the loss of my mother weighed heavy on my heart. I didn't let it show as much and I learned to cope, 'cause like my dad said: it was time to be a man. No matter what, I still had to be Thomas Barnett – attractive, popular, senior, starting-five running back of the Parralin High Jaguars - strong, determined, and strong-willed as my mom would have wanted me to be and as my father wanted me to remain. I felt I had cried like a little girl more than I wanted to and as much as God knows I love my mom, I knew she wasn't gone and she could never be, because she was alive in my heart. So after a couple months on I.R., the beginnin' of April rolled around and I was back on my game, for the most part, with my Jordan b-ball shoes and my fresh Hollister tees.

I was walkin' down the hallway with some of the boys from the squad at school one day, mindin' my own, when this little sexy voice interrupted our conversation. "Boy, you gotta be the finest dude in Orlando."

I slowly turned around to see something that almost made my day; it was Natasha Beckford, a sexy little thing from my Spanish class, who I loved to flirt with. That day, her tight little body was still oh-so-evident in her form-fittin' jeans and I still remember how sexy I thought she was in her baby blue tank top – the same baby blue tank top that was low-cut and showed half of some of the most beautiful...

"What's up?" I couldn't help but to stare at anything but her face; I hadn't seen her curves in a couple weeks 'cause she hadn't been in class for a while and even if she had been, she would've been the last thing on my mind. But at that moment, her tight little frame was and I totally forgot my friends were there.

She licked her full lips and tossed back her long black hair. She must've known I was starting to get excited. I didn't really mean to but I could feel my thoughts drifting to a fantasy about her. "Can I borrow him for a minute, boys?" Her cat eyes broke my chain of thought and I guess my boys got the picture, 'cause they were gone by the time I turned around. I looked back and she seemed a little closer than before – so close I could smell her perfume. "I missed you these past few weeks; you don't call me anymore." I called her a couple weeks before my mom passed, but I was trying to keep whatever we had at a certain level; I would say I didn't too much want it to go past flirting for Danielle's sake, but I'm not really sure that was the reason, at the time.

"I guess you can say I been kinda busy." I couldn't get over how much I wanted to taste how soft her skin was. All I know is, I almost felt like her eyes were burning through me.

"Yeah, I heard about your mom. It must be really rough, but if you need anything – *anything* - I'm here for you." She looked me right in the eyes and the way she said "anything," I knew she wasn't too concerned with my mother's death, but I let that go. I knew she was just trying to get me hot (and it was workin'). All I could do was smirk and grin a little bit to hide the fact that I wanted her, no matter how bad that might seem.

"Oh really." I knew I sounded sexy as I looked her over again, but after I said it, she seemed to tense up a little bit like she saw something behind me that kinda scared her; I didn't pay any mind to it.

"Most definitely." All of a sudden she looked down, blushed and giggled, which was understandable 'cause you could cut the lust between us with a knife. "But, um...don't be a stranger, sexy." She patted my face and slid her fingers slowly over one of my cheeks before she headed down the hall and I watched her from behind sayin', "All right."

I practically had to pick my mouth off the ground before I noticed someone starin' at me out the corner of my eye. When I finally turned my head away from Natasha, I couldn't do anything but laugh; I was definitely busted.

"Don't laugh. You know I hate when you do that, Thomas!" She was yellin' at me from her locker next to mine, as usual. She looked pretty, that day, like she always did, and she was even cuter when she tried to be mad at me.

By the look on her face, I could tell a smile wasn't gonna get me out of it. Then I realized it was that same sour look behind my back that scared Natasha. She always made sure no other girls except Danielle were in my "bubble," as she called it, and she had been looking out for me that way since we met in elementary. Marissa Hall was the only girl I had ever been "just friends" with and the only woman in my life, other than my mother, who I really listened to. She was smart, funny, sweet, and understood me like no dude friend I ever had. Everybody in school thought we were perfect for each other and that we would end up together for sure, 'cause if I wasn't with Danielle, I was with her. But although I had always thought she was a pretty girl, I knew she would never be more than a sister to me.

"I'm sorry, Mommy; it won't happen again." It was so hard not to smile and laugh at her with her stern face and her hand on her hip.

"Don't you always say that, Tom? I don't know when you're gonna be able to keep your eyes to yourself, and your dirty thoughts." She slammed her locker as I remembered all the times she scolded me about being faithful, keepin' at least a B-average in Chem class, and not saggin' my pants too low.

"Come on, 'Rissa; there's nothin' wrong with flirting. Besides, you know these girls come to me. I can't help it if I'm attractive." We started walking down the hallway and I just knew I was gettin' on her nerves.

"And that's your problem, Thomas! One of these days, one of these girls you so-called flirt with is gonna tempt you and you'll be hurt when it all leads to who-knows-where-else, 'cause Danielle is a good girl and she takes a lot off you, but I know for sure she won't take you cheatin' on her." We were outside my Spanish class by then and I almost lost my balance laughin' at her. She thought she knew me so well.

"So that's what this is all about. Listen, my sexy little friend, I can have any girl in this school without even looking twice at her, 'Rissa, so if I wanted to cheat on Danielle, I would have already; don't you think?"

I could tell she had to pause real quick before she went on, all serious. "I think I know you well enough to know that everyone has their weaknesses and even *you* make mistakes."

She almost got me for a second, but I wouldn't let her. "Not that kind, Ms. Hall, but thanks for the lecture." I slapped her butt and disappeared into my class, before she could scream: "THOMAS!"

That conversation really made me laugh and I was still thinkin' about it when I was on my way to lunch. Marissa always had a funny way of making the things that she said stick and it annoyed the hell outta me, especially if she was right. I shook it off as soon as I saw Danielle in the caf. She had on my favorite jeans and her hair was down just how I liked it; that pretty much occupied all my thoughts. I walked up behind her and kissed her on her neck while her friends giggled. She smiled and told them she would talk to them later, as she stood on her tippy-toes to kiss me back.

"Hey, baby!" she was always so excited to see me and I loved the way her kisses were so warm. Like I said, I was comfortable with her and that's what I liked.

I was smilin' really hard by the time we made it to a table and I can remember just staring into her pretty eyes before I asked her how she was doing. "Really good, now that you're here." That was always her answer, but as I slid my hand into her bag of Fritos, I knew there was more to it today.

"What's up, babe; you're up to somethin'" I couldn't decide if it was the fact that she was smiling so much or not, but I knew it was something; I just couldn't put my finger on it.

She stopped smilin' for a second and her face turned a little serious on me and I started to tense up a little bit. "Baby, how do you feel about us?" Just that quick, there was THE QUESTION. My whole facial expression changed, 'cause I remembered how many times Danielle had asked me that question. Every few months after we had been dating five months, she had asked me the *same* thing and it frustrated me *every* time.

"Aw, man. Do you we have to do this today?"

"*Do we have to do this, today?* Thomas, you always avoid it and I wanna know!" I was glad it was loud in the cafeteria, or else I would've been pissed off that she was starting to get loud. For some reason, this time she asked, it felt different. This time, she had a little fire in her eyes and a tone in her voice that I didn't like.

I was so tired of that question and I couldn't understand why she kept askin' it for nothin' in the world. "Why you always gotta go there, Danielle?"

Suddenly she stood up and I remember thinkin' I had never seen her so mad since we had been together. I noticed people were beginning to stare and that pissed me off, too. "*Why do I always have to go there, Thomas! Why do I always have to see where your head is? Because you never tell me!*"

Then I had had enough. I just couldn't see why she always had to push my buttons and why she had to make me repeat the fact that I would rather not talk about that kind of stuff, over and over again. "Danielle, you're makin' a scene!" I stood up in front of her and she could really tell I wasn't havin' it.

"You think I care what these people think! Well, I don't, Thomas! You never tell me how you really feel about us, which means you may as well not even care about this relationship and not even care about me!" She started towards the double doors of the caf as I just stood there.

I saw a lot of people that I knew in my lunch period and she had embarrassed me so much that I didn't even know if I wanted to chase after her. I looked around one last time, noticing Marissa starin' from the distance and decided I wasn't gonna let her get away, especially since I didn't say what *I* had to say.

By the time she had just gotten outside the cafeteria, I yanked her by the arm and my face was starting to turn red. "So you just walk out when you're done, Danielle? What the hell is your problem, girl!"

She shook her arm away from me and I could tell she was just as mad as I was. She looked like she was about to cry. I could always tell, but I didn't pay attention to it; I was too mad. "You're my problem, Thomas! I can talk to you about anything. You're my boyfriend and my best friend and I can really be myself with you. We've been together for over a year and even when we broke up we couldn't live without each other. I love you, Thomas!." I hadn't heard her say those words like that before. Actually, I had only heard those words, once, the summer before when we had had a similar argument about the same thing and I had avoided the expression like she had never said it. But, I heard it that time and there was no way around it.

"I love you and I just don't see why you can't admit that you do, too – or at least try to love me back!"

What she said hit me like a brick wall and I can't really remember too many times that someone had knocked the wind out of me with just something they said. I had been knocked all around the field by the biggest seniors in the state, but I don't think I had ever felt so speechless in my teenage life. "Baby..." I really didn't know what to say. I couldn't change who I was or the way I had always been and I didn't think I was wrong for my decision to keep things the way they were – the way I liked it or was comfortable with. "Baby, you know I care about you." All I could do was look into her pretty eyes and hope she would understand.

"Well, that's not enough for me anymore, Thomas." Tears were spilling out of her eyes and I was starting to feel sick just seeing her cry. "It's not enough."

She didn't look at me for more than a couple seconds longer before she turned around and stormed down the hallway; all I could do was watch her walk away and wonder if she was walkin' out on me all together.

It's hard for me to admit it, but what Danielle had said earlier that day really upset me and I was feelin' it for the rest of the day. I was confused and I couldn't figure out if I was supposed be a little hurt or actually kinda scared...or worried she was gonna leave me. I still couldn't bring myself to feel wrong for my decision and everything, but what she said did make me think a little about what we *did* have goin' on and just what *did* I really want.

"What's up witcha man!" All of a sudden I almost fell off the bench in the locker room. Yet again, someone had caught me off guard but this time the whole squad was in there. We were getting ready for practice and Big Ben knocked me in the chest so hard I almost screamed like a lil girl.

"Nothin', man! Why you always gotta do that!" I got up a little annoyed and started strappin' up.

"Take it easy on 'em, Ben. The wifey's givin' him a hard time." Kevin started laughin' a little and that reminded me about how Danielle was so loud at lunch, all over again.

"You and Danielle goin' at it *again*?" I sat down again to put on my shoes while I looked down to ignore 'em. He just couldn't get the memo that I didn't wanna talk about it. "Listen, Barnett, don't let that girl get your jock strap all in a bunch! There's a party this weekend; we should be celebratin'." He slapped me on the shoulder and a little grin came to my lips.

I had totally forgotten all about the 'Spring Fling' at Ashley G's house; she had it every year, towards the end of April to give us something to look forward to before her big summer bash after graduation. It was hardly on my mind after fightin' with Danielle, though, so I just put on a fake smile, sayin', "Yeah, that's right," while my boys started bets about who was gonna get drunk or laid, first, that weekend.

In the middle of it all, Kevin noticed my facial expression while I could barely get my shirt on and whispered to me, "Girls come and go, Barnett; they're like a good game of foosball: great while it lasts, but they'll be another game next weekend." I just smiled and *tried* to laugh. I had had enough of them seein' me down.

The next few days went by pretty fast. I hardly saw much of Danielle and when I did, we barely said hey to each other and would end up going our separate ways. I hate to say it, but I was really trying to avoid bumpin' into her. I figured I wouldn't know what to say to her anyways, so it was better just to leave it alone all together. It just made it a little difficult, 'cause I kept thinkin' of how disappointed in me my mom would be if she had still been alive – how much she would've given me the evil eye about it and threatened to withhold my allowance until I begged for Danielle's forgiveness. Either way it goes, I threw myself into football harder than ever that week to keep my mind off her and by the time Friday night came around, I felt I had almost gotten over what was said in the argument and seein' her cry. It was just too bad I would see her at the party.

Me and my crew met up at Kevin's house and rode together. I have to admit, all of us looked too good and I was ready to dance with almost any sexy little thing that would keep my mind off of Danielle and luckily when we got there, the room was filled with nothin' but options. The music was bangin' out the house and even though I walked in with about eight dudes, all the girls seemed to be lookin' at me while I made my way to get a beer from Ashley's fridge. *She* was even sexy herself that night in her lil tight pink dress, so when she asked me to dance, I couldn't resist. The lights got low when we startin' dancin'; she was all on me and I just let her do her thing for a while until the song switched and Natalie wanted to dance - and then Tasha and Lexy and Aundrea and Stacy and half the other girls in the room. About an hour into the party, I was exhausted and Ashley's couch was lookin' really good.

"Wooooh! Some party, huh, Tom!" Kevin was lookin' half-drunk screamin' at me from across the room, while some girl was grindin' all on his crouch. I couldn't help but to crack up. "Ha! You're smilin' now, but wait 'till Danielle gets here." Just hearing the name made my stomach flip a little, but not as much as what he said next. "Speakin' of the devil." Boy, I thought I was gonna piss my pants and I couldn't figure out if it was because of how good she looked or if I was actually scared, surprised, and anxious to see her, all at the same time - but mostly the last two. Kevin thought the look on my face was so amusing, but I didn't think the situation was that funny, especially 'cause as soon as she got there she seemed to locate me right away. I tried to act like I didn't see her, but once she was standin' in front of me with her little white skirt, hills, and tube top, I couldn't even act like I didn't notice her.

"Hey," was all she said and the next thing I knew, we were outside staring at each other from across Ashley's backyard veranda. The silence was killin' me for a minute but that didn't last long. She said, "I missed you, Thomas," and that was just the phrase I didn't want to hear – the one that made me melt and almost drop my guard all together.

"I missed you too." That's all I could think of, 'cause I did miss her - just not the complications and all.

"I just didn't. I just don't understand why it's so hard for you."

"Why what is so hard?" I knew what she was talkin' about but I just didn't wanna go there.

"Us, Thomas. Our relationship." I remember thinkin': *Here we go with this again.* I really wanted to enjoy the party without all the drama, but then I realized somethin'.

"You know what, Danielle? This relationship isn't hard for me. I actually enjoy it without all the drama you tend to make." I got a little closer as I said it and she seemed to get a little ticked.

"*The drama*, Thomas? Is that what I do – cause drama?" She was startin' somethin' again, but I was really trying to control myself.

"What do you call it, Danielle – when you keep bringing up the same situation when we've had the discussion before and you know how I feel about it?"

"I didn't know it was such a crime to love someone, Tom."

"I didn't say that, Danielle!" I lost my cool a little bit. "But there is somethin' wrong with you trying to force someone to feel something that they don't!"

For a second I almost regretted what I said, but I didn't know why and just before I caught myself wishin' I could take it back for an unknown reason, she walked right up to me, cornered me and looked directly into my eyes so pointedly, I noticed or thought about nothin' else. "So does that mean you don't love me, and you probably never will?"

*Damn.* I stared at her for a long while, not knowin' what to say; I always hated how she could make me so speechless but want to say so much at the same time. But I thought about the question for a little while and really thought about *everything* and it all added up to, "I think I care for you and that should be enough."

Her face turned frozen and instantly I could see the hurt in her eyes while they filled with tears again. "Well, that answers my question. I'll talk to you later, baby." It was barely a whisper but I heard it as well as the sound of her hills on the pavement leading back into the house.

"Danielle!" was all I screamed while she disappeared back into the party but that time, I didn't chase her; whether I really wanted to or not, *I* only know now.

By the time I had gotten back into the party, everyone seemed like they were dazed. It was dark except for the strobe lights in the center of the ceiling, but I hardly noticed any of it. All I wanted to do was get a beer and get back to the couch; I was so glad no one could see my face because they probably would've guessed all I was thinkin and going through. I sucked back the first beer like a glass of water and then I thought about Danielle and I had another. Then I thought about her crying and what she had asked me, beforehand, and then I had another. Twenty minutes later, I had had four and I couldn't see anybody in the room. I put my head down for a second and covered my face with my hands but when I opened my eyes, I saw the *last* person I needed to see, comin' right towards me. I was so wasted, but even that couldn't keep me from noticin' how fine she looked; all I saw was a red dress and a pair of legs that almost made me drop my Miller Lite.

My beer goggles were clear enough for me to see who she was and by then, she was right in my face with her red lips, long curls, and body to trade your left arm for.

"Hey, you." The tone in Natasha's voice said that she didn't notice or didn't care how drunk I was. I'm sure I had a dazed look on my face and my eyes were low, but not low enough not to notice her shape in the dress she had on.

"What's up, Natasha?" The dudes around me started to laugh as I smiled (probably just because I was stupid drunk). By then, Danielle was the last thing on my mind and I could barely remember my middle name. *Chucky. Charlie. Charles! That's it.*

"Let's dance." She didn't even give me a chance to answer as she pulled me up off the couch and the empty beer can fell on the floor. I had just started to think that somebody really had it in for me, sendin' that girl to that party at that certain time. I already had enough on my mind, but by then, she was dancin' so close to me I could almost feel what kind of underwear she had on. A part of me wanted to tell her I needed to sit back down, but my vision and my thoughts were so clouded, I didn't even see the point and I was so mad with Danielle (and a bunch of other things). I didn't even care anymore, so I just got closer to her, grabbed her hips, and enjoyed it.

By the time we had danced to a few songs, I was so excited and drunk and a few other adjectives I couldn't possibly have thought of at the time, that I didn't know what was goin' on. All of a sudden I was just horny and this fine piece of somethin' was whispering, "Let's get out of here" in my ear and we were on our way to Ashley G's guest bedroom.

I don't remember much, 'cause, like I said, I was DUMB stupid drunk but I know I caught myself thinkin': *O man! What am I doin?* But either way, I kept on walkin' and before you could say *Danielle* I was on the bed of Ashley G's guest bedroom and all Natasha had on was a flaming red bra and some matching lace underwear. My eyes were so big on that bed (and so was somethin' else) and I found myself hoping she couldn't tell how much my guard was let down. I never told a soul until now, but I was scared outta my pants by the time she started crawlin' towards me on the bed but I couldn't control how I felt about how good she looked in her lingerie. Danielle popped into my head once but mostly I heard Marissa and what she had said to me outside my Spanish class the other day. *Damn! Why is she always so right?* But I still wasn't thinkin' straight (that's what five cans of *Miller*'ll do to you) and my body was beginning to take over. Once I thought, *Are me and Danielle even over? Probably not, but I don't' know...*but it was too late, 'cause Natasha was kissing on my neck and my shirt was already off.


"I know you've been wanting this, Tom. I see it in your eyes every time we talk." In my head I was screamin' *NO, I DON'T; STOP!* But the words never came out of my lips and hers looked so good when she said that. I looked into her cat eyes – the same ones that had **ALWAYS** tempted me before - I thought about me and Danielle and all of our arguing, and then I let my hands glide down Natasha's body; somethin' came over me and I kissed those lips stained with cherry red and it was over from there. Just that quick.


I was running water in the sink to wash my face and I caught myself stunned, lost in another world, and caught in a web of about fifteen thoughts. I sure as hell wasn't admiring the skills it took to coordinate the colors of the toilet and the marble, in and around the sink; my mind was somewhere else. I don't really think I knew what was goin' on, at that point. I was kinda blank and I was just there staring and staring, as drunk as can be.


"Hey, you. You got in here so fast, I thought you didn't like it..." A pair of hands slid around my waist and the voice sounded familiar... *Didn't like what?* was all I thought and I remember thinkin' about how pretty the voice was as my eyes slowly began to raise to the position of the mirror...and there she was. She hadn't put all her clothes back on yet, so I had to catch myself from admiring her figure again. I caught myself just in time. *Natasha! Damn.* Then it came back to me, as I crashed back down to earth and my whole body froze. I just stared at her in the mirror and I couldn't feel anything. My mind went to a million places in thirty seconds and I was caught between *Oh my God!* and *What did I do?* I was almost pleading with my memory for some advice from somebody on what to do next – some crazy story from my mom or somethin' else Marissa had said - but I got nothin'. I wanted my mom to pop out of the linen closet and whisper something in my ear that would help me, but she didn't; she wasn't there.


"I gotta go." Suddenly my head was pounding, when I ran out the door of the bathroom like my life depended on a touchdown in a game I wasn't even playin'. I heard her screamm "Thomas, what's wrong?" when I had reached the door and my hand rested on the knob. The only reason I stopped was because it was like my drunkenness had almost disappeared, enough for me to replay in my head all the things I had just done in that room with that girl – like I was tryin' to leave it behind. That just made me furious, 'cause I knew I couldn't, so I just swung the door open; I had to get out.


244

It wasn't any better on the outside. My heart pounded faster in my chest when I saw the *whole* squad back away from the door and a few other people behind them. They had been listenin' to the whole thing and my anger instantly took over me when they cheered for me (to them I had just scored one of the sexiest girls in school and that was that). I didn't even grin lookin' at them so it probably didn't surprise 'em when I immediately stampeded through the party, lookin' for the door. But, that was the last thing on my mind - them and everybody starin' at me - when I ran full speed out the door of Ashley G's house and took off down the street. I had a terrible headache by then and my mind was everywhere, and I kept thinkin' about Danielle. The guilt got worse and worse and I ran faster. Every time her face popped into my head, it got worse and I ran harder.

Just when I couldn't take it and was out of breath, I looked back and realized just how far I had run. The miles flew right past my ears. I looked up and saw I had run all the way home. Then, I ran right into the front door and up to my room with sweat drippin' down my face and shoulders. I didn't even notice my dad sittin' on the couch readin' a book in the living room or the fact that he had said "Son! What the hell?"

I just bolted up the stairs, slammed and locked the door, sat on my bed and started starin' off into space again. It all sank in on me like a pile of bricks weighing down on my head. It was 1:30 in the morning. I had just come back home from one of the hottest parties of that year. I had the worst migraine of my life. By morning I would have a terrible hangover - and most importantly, I had cheated on my girl and by Monday, it would be all over school and we would be over FOR GOOD.

I must've slept through the rest of that entire weekend. My dad never bothered me 'cause I guess he put two and two together and thought I was drunk or high. I guess that's what explained my frantic dashin' up the stairs after the party. Maybe I was hallucinating. My dad was too careless at the worst of times – too careless for his own good and sometimes others'. Either way, I don't remember getting outta my bed for anything but food to puke back up in the toilet. I had a killer hangover and people called my phone non-stop until Sunday night, but I didn't notice. I was out cold. I figured there was nothin' worth gettin' up for anyways, after all that had had happened Friday. I didn't want to think about it or anything else. But when my alarm went off Monday morning, I was forced to get outta bed and as soon as I did, a train-full of thoughts came at me all at once.

I swear I got ready for school that day so slowly somebody could've baked three cakes in the time it took me to put my sneaks on. There was no enthusiasm behind anything I did and that was the only time in my teenage life that I can recall not looking in any mirrors. (I don't even think I brushed my hair). I was too afraid to see my mom's disappointed look – the one I wished I had seen at the party that night, before I...You know how they say the dead can come to you and speak to you - that you'll never really lose the ones you love, because they can come back to you? Well, one of my thoughts was one of anger and spite. My mom didn't tell me anything. She didn't warn me not to go to that party that night. She didn't warn me not to go into the guest bedroom at Ashley's G's, and she didn't warn me not to have sex with Natasha. Since the funeral, she hadn't even popped in to say she loved me or hey or anything. That's only a small percentage of what I thought of on my way to school that day.


        I stared at the letters that spelled out my school's name for a long time, before I even thought about gettin' outta my Honda. I felt like I was on enemy lines and if I got outta the car I would instantly be bombarded by a gang of bullets. I gulped so hard as beads of sweat began to form on the back of my neck, right before I wiped 'em away, thinkin' of what my dad would say about me bein' a scary rabbit. That was the only thing that made me bite the bullet and get outta my car. As soon as I got out, people started to stare and talk in their own little crews while I headed for the doors of the school. I felt like a freshmen, walkin' with my eyes straight down, but once I got to those double doors, I knew I was a dead man walkin'. Seein' the tan-colored marble of the hallways beneath my feet, my heart jumped six inches outta my chest. Everybody seemed to be in the hallway, that day. It was just what I had feared. They were all waiting for me to show up like some reality TV show. *Everybody* knew...*What did I do?*


        On my way to my locker, I tried so hard to keep a straight face and regain my composure, but that was hard 'cause every step drove me closer and closer to my breaking point. The whispering and the starin' was drivin' me crazy and I found myself wanting to run home like a lil geek who got jumped by the football team. Then, I realized how many times I had done that with my crew and I saw them comin' towards me from way down the hall, so I just ran to my locker, grabbed my books, and ran the other way to my class, actin' like I didn't see 'em. They were the last people I wanted to see, that mornin'.


By the time lunch rolled around, I felt like a spy, dodgin' and duckin' around corners. At first, I didn't really know what I was doin', but as I sat in the library (a place I prolly hadn't been since sophomore year) during lunch, I realized I was avoiding Danielle but I couldn't exactly figure out why. *Man what's the deal? Am I scared to run into her? What's the worst she can do? I know it's probably over between us...I think.*


"Hey." I nearly fell outta the chair I was in, when I heard the voice and I couldn't even look at her, once I realized who it was. I stood up so fast you would've thought she was a cop, but she wasn't – just the girl that I shared one crazy night with – one that might've caused repercussions I still didn't even know the extent of.


I sighed long and hard and I was sure everyone thought I was a coke addict on withdrawal or somethin' by the way I kept lookin' around and scratchin' my neck. I was too frantic to even say: "What's up?" I had already turned my feet to walk away.


"Some party, huh? We had fun, didn't we?" Natasha was such an unbelievable girl to me, at that point, and I found myself wonderin' how she could be so calm - how she could smile after all that had happened? *That's right – you don't have a boyfriend. You're just the trick that seduced me into sleepin' witchu for your own selfish reasons and is prolly gonna cost me my girl. Well I'll be damned if you see me sweat. I can be careless too.*

"I'll catch you later, Natasha." I started to walk away, as she called my name, askin' me where I was going. Her voice didn't even faze me anymore and I didn't even wanna think about that night, how she looked naked, or even her name. I was pissed as hell, then I saw Marissa leaving the library and it almost brought a smile to my face; she would make it all better. I didn't know if she was one of the people who called me, over the weekend, 'cause I still hadn't checked my phone. I didn't really care to and I had too much else on my mind.

"'Rissa, wait up!" I almost ran across the library, while some teacher shhhh'd me; nothing else was on my mind except talkin' to my best friend. I knew, when all else failed, Marissa would be there for me and I just *had* to talk to her.

I figured she didn't hear me 'cause she was makin' her way down the hallway, by the time I got to the door, but when I called her again I realized she had and had just kept walkin'. I thought she was just messin' with me, but when I called her two more times she didn't even turn around. I didn't think it was funny at all. I was pretty messed up, by then and had no time for jokes. I bet I looked really desperate chasin' her like that, so before she could turn the corner, I caught up to her and patted her on her back.

"Rissa, didn't you hear me?" All of a sudden she turned around and I saw the look I had seen so many times. She was mad - no, upset and disappointed - and those two were even worse with her. And boy, did I feel it when she looked at me.

"What do you want, Thomas?" I saw a little fire in her eyes and her voice was so serious, the first time I opened my mouth I could barely get the words out.

"Wh...I just wanted to talk to you...What's wrong?" Then it hit me; she wasn't at the party that past weekend, but maybe she had heard some rumors. She wasn't the type to believe that stuff, but maybe it was believable to her. *Man, I really screwed up.*

"The question is, Thomas, what the hell is wrong with *you?*"

"What are you talkin' about, 'Rissa?" I was really shocked at how she was talkin' to me. I don't think I had ever seen her *that* mad. But at the same time, I was searching to see if she had heard or not. I knew she was in the ballpark. She just hadn't taken the first swing, yet...

"Don't play stupid with me Thomas!" then her tone changed. "But you gotta be stupid to do what you did on Saturday, don't you?" She was patronizing me and I didn't like it, but I couldn't really defend myself. "Did you have fun at the party, my best buddy ol' pal?"

I looked away for a second and noticed people were starting to look a lil bit, but then my attention came back "Marissa, why you trippin'? You don't have to clown me in the hallway like this..." That's all I could think to say.

"You know what, Thomas? You're worried about the wrong thing, just like always! But you're right, sweetie; I *don't* have to clown you in the hallway this way, because you clowned yourself when you decided to screw Natasha at that party this weekend and I sure hope it was worth it." Her tone changed again – this time to a tone of true disappointment and almost disgust. She stepped in closer to me and leaned towards my ear, as she lowered her voice. "I don't know if you've noticed, Tom, but Danielle is not at school today, which means she is probably at home, crying her eyes out over you and your idiocy. You've probably broken her heart and totally lost her trust. And you know what, Tom? You have also defied mine." I was frozen in that spot for at least sixty seconds before I watched her start to walk away. The words I couldn't find to say, stuttered in my mind. It was a slap in my face; she was supposed to help me, not...

"'Rissa, how do you even know that I did it?"

She turned around, took a few steps back, looked me right in my face and looked just like my momma did when she wanted to know the real truth. "Did you, Thomas Barnett?" I didn't say a word. I just stared at her with eyes that didn't allow me to hide anything or make sure nobody could read what I truly felt. I couldn't do that with Marissa and she knew it. "I thought so."

She disappeared down the hallway and I felt like someone had just told me I had cancer. Her words stung me so hard I couldn't keep it from showing. I remember thinkin' how stupid my response was, feelin' so stunned and just shocked into silence – no funny remarks or jokes or cute smiles could get me outta that one. And then I found myself wonderin' if there was a possibility that I had just lost my best friend.

That was one of the hardest school days of my senior year. I didn't even go to football practice - that should explain it all. I still couldn't believe Marissa did me like that at school and her words kept replaying in my head like a scratched record, as I drove home. But she was right; I didn't see Danielle all day and more people with no lives told me she was at home. Some said she was sick with the Ebola virus after I had forced her to go to Africa and planned to run off with her best friend. Others said we got into a fight at Ashley G's party because she had AIDS and I was disgusted and left her for Natasha, but I knew the truth, or at least I thought I did.

I thought about it all the way home and I even tried to brush it off when I got there. But there were no good afternoon shows on and I had been through all my Playboy magazines - enough for a whole lifetime. I even did my homework, cleaned the house from top to bottom (somethin' my Dad had been tryna to get me to do for weeks), and rearranged my bookcase in alphabetical order, but even that wasn't enough. After hours of stuff like that, I was sittin' on the bed holding my phone just starin' at her number in my contacts list. By then it was nine, my dad still wasn't home and wouldn't be for hours, so the entire house was silent and all I could hear were my thoughts and my sighs.

*....I shouldn't even waste my time 'cause she isn't even gonna pick up...I prolly wouldn't....* Then out of no where I heard the phone ringin' in my ear; I had found the strength to call her....*Come on pick up, girl.....At least I'm tryna call...* "Hi, it's Danielle. Can't make it to the phone right now, so leave me a message and I'll hitchu back. Thanks." I had gotten the voicemail after two rings and my heart rate shootin' up the wall. *Maybe it was an accident or she was talkin' to her mom.* I waited a couple minutes and tried again. I was startin' to feel like I really wanted to talk to her. It was like waiting for paternity test results, waitin' for her to pick up. Her phone rang once...twice...three times...four...five...but who was I kidding? She wasn't gonna pick up, she wasn't talkin' to me. *I guess she's really mad, this time.*

My heart sank as I hung up and took a deep breath. Suddenly I found myself so glad my dad wasn't there to see my face. How I felt was indescribable. I think I was actually...hurt. I took a shower and went to bed early, that night; that day had been a rough one for me. I figured since Danielle wasn't answerin' her phone and Marissa straight called me out at school and *WALKED AWAY*, somethin' she had NEVER done to me EVER before in our ENTIRE friendship, it was the beginning of a lonely week or maybe more. And there was still no sign of my mom...

Over the next few days, I probably paid more attention to the color paint on the walls than I did my teachers. The Tuesday after she yelled at me, I found out Marissa had changed lockers with somebody else on the other side of the school. When I found out I was next to some short freshman with braces, I just turned and walked away in disbelief. I was so numb it was ridiculous, but I put on a good front for the school and my football "buddies," who were still talkin' about how good I hit Natasha. If only they knew (I got annoyed just listenin' to 'em, so I just went to practice and skipped out as soon as possible). I didn't talk to my dad when I actually saw him after school, the first half of the week, and by Thursday when he finally asked me if anything was up, I just blew him off and went to my room. Danielle hadn't come to school at all so far that week and I can't count the times I attempted to call her again, but my pride wouldn't let me do it - no matter how much I missed her or wondered if we were *really* over or thought about her pretty smile, her hugs, her kisses, I just *couldn't* do it. But Friday, everything changed.

I had just given the freshman at my locker an ugly look when she asked me for an autograph, when I turned to walk away and saw her walkin' with her friends. Danielle looked better to me then than she did in the entire time we were datin'; she had on a long white dress and her hair was pulled back into a bun. My heart jumped and she hadn't seen me yet, but something about her pulled me to her like a magnet. I had forgotten about that whole weekend, the last few days, my pride, the risk - everything. All of a sudden, I was moving towards her and I couldn't stop.

"D...Danielle" her friend had walked away and she was looking down, textin'.

"What's up?" She hadn't looked up yet, so I guess she figured it was somebody else. When she finally did look up, I instantly wished I hadn't come over; it was the first time I had seen her eyes in a week and her eyes burned right through me. "Get the hell away from me!" I felt like I had just gotten shot and she started to walk away so fast it was almost a jog.

It set me off course for a second, so it took me a minute to react and **EVERYBODY** in the hallway was whisperin' and lookin' (that was the moment they all had been waiting for). "Danielle, wait!" She had made some distance from me, so I was trying to catch up. She never turned around and she was movin'.

She turned the corner and I was gainin' on her. All I heard her say was, "I have nothing to say to you, Thomas!" I was runnin' then 'cause she was almost out of reach. I could barely form my mouth to say "Stop" and before I knew it, I was out of breath and had grabbed her arm. Then she surprised the hell outta me with somethin' that knocked the wind out of me, literally. She turned around and with one hand, slapped me so hard I stumbled back a foot. "Don't you dare touch me, you selfish bastard!"

I was in total shock and my face was burnin' like a bottle of IcyHot. "What the hell is wrong with you?" was all I could think to say, even though I knew the answer and I knew I was dead wrong for what I had done to her.

"Are you serious, Thomas!" Everybody was lookin'; she was livid and right in my face. "If you know what's good for you, you'll stay

255

away from me! You've embarrassed me and hurt me more than you will ever know! I gave you everything I had, Tom..." she instantly started crying, and the tears stung me more than her hand did.

"Baby, I..."

"Shut up! I waited a whole week to say this! You are a lying, cheating, stupid, immature little boy, who doesn't know what he had and now it is gone! You need to grow up and get some sense about yourself before you break more hearts and ruin more good things! As for me, we are done, *for good!* I hate you, Thomas Barnett and if I ever see you again in my life, it will be too soon! Forget my name, forget my number." Tears fell to the floor while her anger increased and I looked at her in awe. "Forget my address, forget all the memories we had together, forget all the TIME I spent on you – forget everything! Stay out of my life and stay out of my face!" That was the second time a girl had walked away from me that week. I was speechless and I didn't even try to say a word. I had my proof. It was over between us; there were no gifts or tears or anything that would get her back, just the whole school staring at me in the hallway and a hurt in my heart that was masked by anger on my exterior...

"What the hell are ya'll lookin' at!" Everybody scattered like roaches and I saw Marissa stunned, standing by her *new* locker, as I stormed down the hallway.

I must've looked like a homeless person, walkin' into my house like a man without a cause. There was no more hiding anything and a big part of me didn't even wanna try. *What just happened today?* I asked myself, but I knew exactly what had happened. Danielle left me and Marissa wasn't even there to be a friend; it was funny, because as I sat my book bag on the floor and plunged onto the couch, I think I might have been more concerned with not only having lost my girl, but my best friend. I couldn't believe that in the course of a week, I had been shut down twice, slapped in public, and humiliated by the girl I had spent the last year and a half with and my best friend of forever.

After a day of feeling nothing but consuming anger, suddenly, on my way home from school, (and after chargin' into a bunch of dudes on the field like they stole my wallet *and* my sneaks) all I ended up bein' was kinda...broken. Nobody was home but I still tried to laugh it off, tryna front but I couldn't. I put my head in my hands and out of nowhere, I felt a ball risin' up in my throat. *Why did I do that!...it didn't even have to go there, that night...and now...* Then I felt angry again out of nowhere – partly angry at the girls, and myself and because I was being a punk, about to cry again. *What the hell is wrong with me?* I was so glad no one was there to see me chopped up like that.

"Son." I spoke too soon. I didn't even hear him come in; he wasn't supposed to be home from work for hours.

"Dad." I hopped up off the couch and wiped my face; there were no tears...*Good.*

"Don't try that with me, boy; sit down." He sat his briefcase down and I felt like I hadn't seen him in days, 'cause I really hadn't, mentally. I slowly sat down and lowered my head a little. "Now, you've been walkin' around for days like some kinda zombie and I know we don't talk much..." he sat down on the couch across from me, "but I think it's about time you tell me what's goin' on."

I took a deep breath, still not really lookin' into his eyes. *Man, should I?*. But then I decided there was nothin' to be ashamed of. After all, he was still my dad and I didn't have to tell him my life story or nothin'. Then, it all came out. I told him the whole story about Danielle - everything that had happened and had been happening in our relationship (some things I had never even told my mom, before) – and about that night at Ashley G's. After that, I told him about how Marissa left me and how I didn't even know if we were friends anymore. Everything came out and when I was done, he silently sat across from me and I sat back with a deep sigh.

His eyes were serious and his face was still and unmoved, so I had no idea what to think. It took a minute for him to start. "Well, son, as you grow older, you'll see that girls come and go and there's really nothin' you can do to make them stay. I mean, you gotta do what you gotta do and be who you are as a man..." *A man? Does a man really cheat on his girl...if so, why is Marissa so mad...what are you sayin' Dad?* "and if girls don't understand that, so be it. Son, you have the right to do whatever you want to do and you can't be ashamed to be young. Personally, at your age, or at any age comin' soon for you, I don't think you did anything wrong. A man is a man and boys *will be* boys."

258

I was silent. *I wonder if he would say that if Mom was here. But, wait a minute! I told Danielle how I felt about us, so she should've known that I was. Not necessarily, but I never forced her to have such deep feelings for me. But Marissa...*

"Listen, Son, don't let these girls get you down; in the end you gotta look out for you. Remember that." He stood up and so did I and we shook on it. It was the first time I had looked him in the eye for days, maybe even weeks; I had a small smile on my face, somethin' I hadn't had for a while. Maybe everything would be all right, after all. He was right. *I am a man and I do as a man does: as he pleases.*

I think, well, I know I took that conversation to the heart, probably more than I even know, now. I spent the whole weekend with my dad's words ringin' in my head. I didn't think of what I did to Danielle; I wasn't worried about havin' my swag a little cramped at school; I couldn't care less about all the arguments and the fights; and I just *knew* that eventually I would get over Marissa. I convinced myself that I was done with it all and by Monday, I had went to a party, snuck into a club, got completely wasted, and then I was walkin' down the hall like a new person, or maybe just the old me, reborn.

I was slowly becoming callous to all that had happened and determined to bring my other side abruptly to the surface – flirt with who I wanted to, look at who I wanted to, have any girl I wanted. I figured I had done all I could and it still wasn't good enough – not good enough for Danielle and not quite there for Marissa – so why even bother anymore? I was gonna do whatever the hell I wanted to and not give a second thought to what anybody thought of it. I was done bein' a punk and lettin' girls mess with my head; it was time for me to live my life and be my own man. *Thanks Dad.*

I probably had about twenty dates within the next month or so and by May I hadn't talked to Marissa or Danielle. I passed right by Danielle in the halls like I didn't know her and Marissa seemed to avoid me, because I hardly ever saw her and when I did, she was across the room or down the hall from me. Natasha spent the night at my house a couple times by prom, but me and the squad decided we were too cool for the dance, so we went to Daytona and spent the weekend at Kevin's dad's beach house, instead. Before I knew it, graduation was right around the corner, and me and my Dad spent more weekends together than we had in my whole life. I had had half the girls on the cheerleading squad in my phone or in my bed. I was on top of the world, oblivious to everything that would bring me off my pedestal. Me and the team finished up the rest of the football season, gettin' accolades at regionals and I was definitely satisfied with being MVP (so was my dad, the suits over at U of F watin' on me, and my coach). It was just too bad my high school career had to come to an end, but I figured college was an even better start. Thomas Barnett was gonna take the University of Florida by a storm, regardless of all that had happened.

*Today's the day.*

"Son."

I was in my room, putting on my cap and gown. It was finally the day to walk across that stage. I was too focused on how good I looked and the legacy I was leaving behind at Parralin to notice my dad standing at my door, let alone his facial expression. "I just wanted to say..."

"Come on, Dad; we ain't got all day." I was crackin' up when I turned around. It was like pullin' teeth with him to open up, even a little; he had a look on his face like I had done something wrong but it was somethin' else – something more important and complicated: expressing himself.

"You...You look good, Son." I knew that wasn't what he really wanted to say, but I still smiled all the way to the school.

The music was starting and I was waitin' behind two other people for my name to be called. My heart started pounding and all the sudden, I found myself thinkin' about my mom and the fact that she wasn't gonna be there. Then, they called my name and pushed the thought from my mind. There was no sense in thinking about what couldn't be. When I grabbed my diploma and turned to smile for the camera, as my principal placed my tassel on the other side of my cap, I felt like that single motion marked the end of high school and everything that had happened there: the high school girls, Danielle, football games, old times with my boys, the break-up, the big party, Natasha, prom, and maybe even Marissa. Too much had happened and I wanted to forget most of it and the people associated with it, if possible. But even though the ceremony was over, we hadn't left the schoolyard yet, which means the show wasn't over.

"Thomas, can I talk to you for a sec?" I was laughin' with my dudes and I immediately thought it was another sexy hopeful, just craving for my number. I turned around with a sexy smile. *Duty Calls.* But, I wasn't expecting it to be Marissa. I hadn't seen her since our fight and it didn't help my cause that she looked absolutely gorgeous with her hair down and fresh face. Truly, my heart almost stopped when I saw her, but after a moment of showing the vaguest of emotion, I turned my head to look off in another direction away from her, like I wasn't concerned – that would've been the old me.

"What's up?" I wasn't even looking into her face, but I could still *see* her.

*Why does she always have to look at me like that?* I could tell what I was doing wasn't phasing her; she was gonna say what she had to say, regardless. "Hi, Thomas..." she paused for a second and looked me right in the face. I darted my eyes quickly towards hers and back in the other direction. She just ignored me; she saw right through every stupid thing I ever did; she always had. She grinned for a second as she went on. "I just wanted to congratulate you and wish you the best of luck in all your future endeavors, Tom." (I hadn't heard that nick name from her, in a while and I blinked really hard, when she said it). "I hope you find everything you wish for, in college and in your life from now on, but don't forget where you've come from. Most of all, Thomas, I hope you make wiser and more intelligent decisions." *Thanks, 'Rissa; STAB me while I'm down.*

I scoffed, still lookin' away. But when she said the last line, I couldn't avoid her eyes any longer. She grabbed my hands in hers and hit me below the belt. "Even though, we have our *great* differences, Tom, I want you to know if you ever *really* need something, you can come find me. I'll miss you, Thomas Barnett. Be good." She smiled and as she turned away, I couldn't help it, but I was breathless. I could barely say, "Okay."

I didn't know what to say....*Wasn't she supposed to be mad at me? Was she just sayin' that to make things right with herself before she walked out of my life?* I started to call her name and the first part came out, but only as a whisper. She was more than ten feet away from me but I had a strong urge to just call her back. *'Rissa don't go! I'm gonna miss you, too...I wish... Let's just start over. I wish I could take it all.* All of a sudden I noticed my friends got quiet behind me and remembered that I was supposed to be on a new swag, so I calmed my thoughts and decided I wouldn't call her back. No matter how much I felt like my heart had instantly shattered or fallen down to my stomach to or no matter how unsure I was if I would ever even see her again (or how long it would be until and if I did) or no matter how much I couldn't stop thinking about how *long* she had been my *best* friend. I regained my composure like a marine after a great war, smirked and turned back around to my boys. Then, I started joking around again like I didn't even care.

The next few weeks after graduation were kinda thoughtful - no matter how much I refused to admit it - but I brushed it off with more dates, parties (including Ashley G's big summer bash), and going to the beach. "My new swag" kinda got to me at times – times that I attempted to call Marissa but just *couldn't* find the strength from anywhere to do it, or times when I passed Danielle in the mall and had to act like I didn't even wanna say hey, or times when I saw my mom's pictures around the house and quickly shoved them outta my view. I didn't wanna have a big party for my birthday in July 'cause I knew the most important person I wanted to be there (Marissa) wouldn't be but I didn't tell my boys that. I just made up some lame excuse and we ended up celebratin' my eighteenth in the VIP room at Club Sway. Afterwards, I spent the night at a hotel with some heavy-chested, hour-glass shaped girl named Candy (after getting smashed until four in the mornin' wit my dudes) and in the mailbox, back at home, I found a check for five-hundred bucks from my Dad and a card from somebody. When I opened it, it was from Marissa; I hadn't heard from her since graduation and I was so pissed she didn't even bother to call me for my birthday that I just threw it away.

I felt myself becoming more careless about things as the days went on 'cause it was easier and it made things simpler - the way I liked 'em. I told myself every day that this was the way it had to be and no matter what had happened, I had to live *my* life. I was the most important person in it and in the end, it was all about me. But after all, I concluded that sometimes it really helped to have your boys to make the days go by with a little more pizzazz, to keep you smilin' instead of frownin', to back you up on pretty much anything

264

you say and help you forget the things you don't really wanna think or talk about.

But the summer could only go by so quick and I was forced to face facts the morning I was set to go to college. It had come all too soon and as I looked at my almost-empty room and tucked the last shirt into my suitcase, a lot of thoughts came rushing back to me like ghosts lurkin' in the shadows. A lot had gone down in that school year, but all I could do was get angry when I thought of it too much, so I was relieved when it was time for me and my dad to head off to my school. *Who wants to sit around havin' a pity party about stuff I can't change? Hell!* I took my stuff to the car and forgot about it all...or tried to.

It didn't help too much that it was a pretty long car ride to Gainesville and it was almost as silent when me and my dad came back from my mom's funeral. That brought a little pain into my system and the silence seemed to mess with me. Somehow, I felt like we were both tryna avoid talkin' about anything, because the truth was, we were all each other had and I was leavin', so it would be the first time my dad would be all alone in the house. *I wonder what he's gonna do without me...and mom?* I don't think he even knew that I caught wind that we were most likely thinkin' about the same things when I glanced at him, as he kept a steady speed on the freeway. His face was serious as usual but I could tell there was something there. *I wish he would tell me how he...Well, we don't really do that, especially not Dad, so I guess I understand.* I guess I looked at him too long or he was trying to avoid what was, 'cause he cracked a joke out of nowhere and there was no more silence for the rest of the ride.

Before I knew it, the laughing came to a halt and nothing was said, by the time we rolled up on the campus. I was kinda upset that Dad had suddenly run out of jokes. I didn't want the

265

silence either. "So…" we spoke abruptly at the same time and my dad brushed it off with a chuckle and I joined in behind him. We were nervous, but neither one us was gonna say it aloud. I looked him in the face and we locked eyes for a second, but then we both looked away. I suddenly felt like I did on my first date (I didn't know what to say to the girl but I really wanted to kiss her) and it was gettin' awkward.

"Let's get your stuff, huh?" He slapped me on my arm and jumped out of the car. I had to hide the fact that I was kinda disappointed for a second but I shook it off and hopped outta the car to get my stuff. We unloaded my bags on the curb pretty quick and then it was back to the silence. I was lookin' down, avoidin' his eyes and all of a sudden I was grabbed into a bear hug. It was so fast I almost screamed like a little girl, but I kept it together 'cause there were people around. I was shocked.

"Listen to me, Son, and listen good"

*I'm listening! I'm listening! Loosen up.*

"You're up here to do one thing and that's get an education. Don't let too much else get in the way of that or your future. You've made me and ya momma so proud already," I hadn't heard him actually say the word *momma* in a while, "and I just know you're gonna be somebody." Then he pulled me away at arm's length and went on for his last statement. (By then, my torsoe was killin' me). "Take care of yourself, boy, and don't you let us down." I didn't really know what to say to that, so I just nodded in agreement – shocked by all he had said - and we slapped our hands together really hard before we shook on it, pounded fists, and then he was gone. As I watched his car pull away, I couldn't help but to feel a jerk at my heart, but I didn't let my face show it – that had quickly become a habitual thing for me; I didn't even have to think about it, anymore.

I turned around to face the school and took a deep breath before I made my way to the stairs leading inside, thinking of what he had said. That time, the words were thoughtful and made a lot of sense but I had mixed feelings. I thought about it all as I checked in, made my way to my dorm, and plopped down on the bed. I was bunkin' with a big dude named Aaron who had been playin' for the Gators for two years already, but I didn't pay him too much mind. All of a sudden I had a lot on my mind and I laid down to look at the ceiling. I was eighteen years old – an adult – out in the world all alone for the first time with no best friends, no mother, and no girl to help me cope a lil better. I had left Orlando and my only connection to *Orlando* (it seemed) - and all I had experienced in just the months that had passed - had sped down the street only moments before.

I didn't know exactly how I felt but it was a mix of a little sadness, worry, anger, fright, apprehension, and excitement. I was excited to be free and a new man, out in the world; angry 'cause my mom wasn't gonna be there to see it and neither was my *so called* best friend; scared outta my pants 'cause I had never done it before; and kinda sad that I didn't even know if I would ever see Marissa again. *Why couldn't Dad just say he would miss me and he loved me?* But when my roomie asked what was up, I just hopped up and said "Oh, nothin', man."

It took me a whole ten minutes to figure out why my leg was throbbin' and developing a bruise, before I looked up and saw this huge 6'4, 256 pound guy hoverin' over me. I turned to see that it was five a.m. and realized he had given me a frog to wake me up. *Great.* "Two-a-days" was all he said, before he

267

heaved a bag of gear and directions at my back. I just plummeted my head back to my pillow. *Day One.*

I was totally out of my element gettin' ready at 5:15 in the morning, and by the time I had walked half way off campus, I just knew something was wrong – I had the directions upside down. I started to wonder what would happen to me, 'cause my roommate left twenty minutes before me; I assumed we were hittin' *our* field at *our* school, but I finally reached my destination at 6:05. There were a couple coaches, but all I could pay attention to was the band of angry players, staring dead at me. I was still almost half asleep but I knew I was in trouble, as an ounce of fear began to rise up my spine. *I hope we're not in too much trouble. Why didn't Aaron tell me where...*

"Good morning, Son. I'm Coach Morrison." Out of nowhere, I felt a slap on my shoulder and looked up to see one of the coaches suddenly standing next to me, looking me dead in the eye. "I'm gonna assume that you had a little trouble findin' our location and all. I would feel safe to say you maybe thought we would be practicin' on the field." I was suddenly too afraid to answer. "I could also rightfully assume you are a freshman and do not know the school just yet. For these reasons, I am not gonna embarrass you, today. Plus, I've heard quite a few great things about'cha. But for future reference..." I was trembling on the inside, listening to his Southern dialect, stern yet calm in my ear. "6 'o' clock, sharp. 5:58, if you're smart. Here, in line, ready to get on the bus. Understood, Barnett?"

I was still afraid to answer him (and that all the dudes would kill me at any moment). "Yes, sir."

"Understood, everybody?" he screamed and I almost flinched. I got in line by my roommate as he quickly turned the

other way. I couldn't shake the look on his face, as we all
answered coach in unison.

Soon, I finally got to see why we weren't practicing on the
field. Coach Morrison and his assistant, Coach Dodge, explained
to us that no one (not even returning players) was a Gator until
they put on their team uniform and stepped on the field for the
first game of the season. They explained that until that
moment, you had to earn every moment of playing time you
received; therefore, we did not yet deserve to embark on the
"sweet, green, plush, turf of U of F" as coach called it. We
drove out to this run-down, abandoned ground a few miles from
school, where the soil was tough and the grass was either dead
or so dry you could scrub a pan with it.

"Here, we will spend the next four weeks we have, before
our first game: bleedin', sweatin', and workin' harder than you
have ever known in your life. And if you have to cry, you better
not let anyone see it, not even yourself. We raise men out here,
so half of you boys will not be here in two weeks because you'll
either quit or wish we would cut ya because your back will ache;
your legs will burn and you just might break somethin'. But one
thing is for damn sure: you will be victorious in EVERY SINGLE
GAME OF THE SEASON, or you will pay for it." *Every game?
What did I get myself into?* "Now, gentlemen, we work."

I took those words too lightly when they first came out of
his mouth, for some stupid reason. I took what he said as a
psyche trip, but by the end of the workout, the only one trippin'
was me. As if the workout wasn't hard enough, the coaches
seemed to be five times harder on us with the excuse that I was
late. By the time we were back at the school locker room, I had
thrown up four times, my body was burning from my forehead
to my left pinky toe, I had a killer migraine, and the whole team
hated me. Somewhere in between collapsing on the bench
outside the shower room and wishing I had never applied for U

of F, I got assaulted for the second time that day; it was my roommate again.

"Thanks a lot, Barnett." Aaron was gettin' some clean clothes out of his locker and glarin' at me every few minutes.

I couldn't believe he had said that, as I slowly raised my body to sit up. *Dude, it's your fault! You should've told me EVERYTHING.* He didn't give me a chance to respond though, so I just gave 'em somewhat of a dirty look – partly because I was kinda scared; the dude was huge. "If you're gonna be a Gator and my roommate, there's two things you gotta know..." everybody around was paying attention by then. "Be on time and don't ever get caught slippin." I suddenly sat all the way up, fighting the pain shootin' through my body; dude was really makin' me feel like a wimp. But then I noticed some other freshman comin' out the bathroom who was skinnier and that made me feel better.

"It's dog eat dog out here, fish. This ain't high school; this here ain't even college; this is Gatorville and when you slack on the team, you got Gainesville and the rest of the South to answer to." Aaron was fully dressed by then, as he leaned right down in my face with a real serious look. "With the Gator boys, you're a celebrity as long as you work hard and stay on top. But when we hit that field, no girls, parties, or video cameras matter. It's just us and the leather gliding off our fingertips and you gotta show up or go home. So man up, Barnett and man up, quick."

Aaron suddenly turned around to leave after that and what he said started to sink in a little. I couldn't help but to feel punk'd or defeated – like I should've said, "Whatever, dude" or somethin' to maintain some kinda level of manhood, but I couldn't, after all. Everybody was staring and had heard everything. "Welcome to Gatorville, Barnett; welcome to THE team," somebody said with a serious tone of warning. I just sluggishly made my way to the shower trying not to limp in front of anybody.

You have never been tired in your life until you've practiced in the scorching, burning heat of the morning for hours, limped back to school to dress for your classes, rushed all around campus to be late for all of 'em, barely made it to the second practice of the day for another three hours, and still had to crack a book open for homework you got on the first day. It only made my muscles hurt more (as I fell unto my bed back in the dorm) to know that I had to do it all again the next day. I had barely been away from Orlando for more than twenty-four hours before I started to feel like I was ready to go home. I was so glad Aaron wasn't there 'cause for a second, I was so exhausted that I fell back into thoughts of the past, really quick. He would've seen me a little broken, tired beyond all means, thinkin' of Marissa, my dad, my mom, and all I had faced and all I was in to face in college and in life from that point on. I was dog-tired - beyond the physical – just thinking of the challenge ahead of me. *Can I really do this, man?* I fell asleep at eight-thirty, fatigued, a tad saddened and knowin' that the next day was day two of *tryna* be a grown man and I was starting to think I wasn't strong enough.

The next few weeks flew by with more unintended thoughts of high school, bustin' my hump tryna juggle school and football, and not seein' much of my roommate, until one Wednesday night when I had come back from the library workin' on a paper, *after* practice. I was sittin' on my bed studying for a psych test when Aaron came in, laughin' on the phone. I cut him a look and then he got off quicker than I could say shut up; then, he just looked at me  strange and then darted across the room, snatching my book away from me.  My first reaction was to cuss 'em out.

"What are you doin', man!"  He screamed at me before he looked at me all disgusted; I could barely answer. *What does it look like?* "Fish, fish, fish, fish!"

"What, dude?" I couldn't take it anymore!

"Barnett, lemme show you somethin'." He practically grabbed me off my bed and led me into the hallway and it was like another world. There was a crowd of the boys from the team and about twenty-seven girls in their bikinis, slippin' and slidin' in the hallway with bubbles smeared everywhere, while I had been studying the difference between the Oedipus and Electra complexes. "Now do you see what I mean?"

I just nodded my head. "Teachers hand us A's; girls hand us their panties; all we have to do is run the school, Barnett." Aaron patted my shoulder. "Work hard, play hard."

That night was the most fun I had had, since prom; I never knew how much fun soap and a hallway could be or just how sexy college women were and that was only the beginning. From then on, there were plenty of parties and perks to college life that bein' a Gator earned you. I quickly came to see that the only place we had to really work was on the field and the rest was basically handed to us. We were on top of the world and it was better than high school in so many ways – everything was bigger and better.  By the time our first game came around, I had lost the "fish" nickname and gained so much respect from the team. Bein' on the Gators' team was like being a celebrity; on TV, they called me "King" because I had become the king of the field and I felt like I ruled the district.

Everything was going well, but by the end of the spring semester, I had to float back down to earth, when I talked to my dad and he told me Marissa was going away to Cambridge to study law at Harvard I didn't want to be hurt but a part of me was; the news  hit me like a brick wall. *She didn't even write to tell me or nothin'. I didn't think she would be leavin' so soon either. Damn.*

I remember the day it happened like it was yesterday; I was out to eat with one of the cheerleaders from our team. I got off the phone with my dad and walked away from the table to the bathroom, ignoring Casey's screaming at me, askin' me where I was going. Without a second thought, I dialed Marissa's cell and I wasn't surprised when there was no answer, even after the third time I called. Then, I got desperate and called her house phone (I guess my new swag went out the window for a minute). *I can't believe she's leavin'.* Her mom picked up and I guess she was startled to hear from me or I caught her off guard because she immediately told me Marissa wasn't home. I wanted to believe her and I did for a minute, but right before I started to tell her bye, I heard Marissa whispering in the background, "Just hang up, Mom." I instantly realized what was going on, as Mrs.  Hall suddenly rushed me off the phone.

My heart sank into my stomach but my face showed nothing at all. As the dial tone sounded in my ear, it sounded like the flat line of the death of me and 'Rissa's friendship. I was suddenly angry and to avoid being sad enough for it to lead somewhere else, I decided I didn't care anymore. I smirked and laughed, walking back to my busty date. *So this is how she wants it. Okay then; Bye Marissa.*

From then on, I crafted myself to be a man of no relents and no regrets. Football was the most important woman in my life and the other ones were merely entertainment. I built a legacy, helping Aaron and the rest of the starting five take our team to state and became victorious. My name was common to Gainesville and beyond, and I was hand-picked the best of everything that an eighteen year-old celebrity college football player could have. I had any girl I wanted in the bed upon a few words if I wanted and I didn't think twice about their feelings – it was all a part of the new me. I had no time for heartache and tears. For the rest of my freshmen year, Marissa was lucky if she even entered my mind for more than a second and I never wrote or tried to find a number to call her. I won't lie and say I never wondered about her but I *wondered* what it would be like to actually earn my A's in school, but that didn't mean I was gonna study. I totally transformed my personality and carried it all the way through college.

It's amazing how fast getting your education flies by when you don't bother yourself with the drama of caring about the past and anything that really makes you work too hard to understand enough to hurt or care. I helped my team get to state every year I played and I always played because I was "King" and MVP (after Aaron left, before my Junior year), who was highly favored and needed, all the way up to my Senior year. I graduated U of F with a bachelor's degree in Business Management and a reputation of being a sexy, cocky football celebrity who anyone was lucky to even get the chance to talk to. I didn't really care that my mom wasn't at my graduation and I didn't bother inviting my dad to be there. All I needed was myself and the self-centered empire that gave me all the joy and prestige I needed...or so I thought.

The only remorse that I experienced from college was that it all seemed to end too quickly, but I didn't have time to care; I got offers to play ball professionally for several teams but turned them all down, because "I played enough ball. What's the point; I'm a Gator. I'm already a star." Instead, fresh outta college, I took a job offer at **Sweat Magazine**, the biggest sports magazine in the country that beats **Sports Illustrated** hands down, with the women and the articles. I moved to Miami and within the next few years, I found myself working towards my most recent position: Vice President of the company. Now, the whole city knows my name: Thomas Barnett, twenty-six year old "King" of the hottest sports magazine there is. I had bought a seven hundred thousand dollar house on Miami Beach, equipped with maids, butlers, three top of the line cars (including my infamous black Jag – 'Midnight'), and the whole nine. My job embodies my lifestyle – anything I want, I get. As VP, I oversee everything and every girl fresh out of high school or denied by Playboy knew they had to go through me to make the magazine and they would do whatever it took – *whatever* it took.

I became a guy of no second chances and first chances that were harder to get than it is to find diamonds in a fish bowl. I had high expectations in my home, with my job and my women; my standards were high, but I was still "King" of my castle and I did whatever I want. This was only less than a year ago, when if I didn't want to go on a date that was previously scheduled I just didn't call to tell the girl; when I slept with whomever I pleased, disappeared to a meeting in the morning, and had the maid show the girl out when she woke up; and when I just *knew* I was the sexiest man alive with all the power in the world and nothing to push him off of cloud nine – not just yet anyways.

I never really ate at home unless I was throwing a dinner party, so I would normally spend my Miami nights with some young, aspiring model or actress grabbin' at a chance to get the next week's cover spread before she resorts to Hollywood. But I

275

remember one particular night pristinely. I was out with this Ford model named Stephanie; I didn't really like her personality but I took her out to Quinn's anyways, 'cause I wanted some company for the night. I was sitting across from her sippin' wine to stay awake before the food got there since she was talking so much it felt like she was auditioning for The View. I would just nod my head every now and then to make it seem like I was listening but soon I was really paying attention, just not to her.

My eyes had instantly darted across the restaurant to a woman far more beautiful than Stef; she was shorter but her skin was closer to mine, her hair longer than Stef's (and natural), and she was wearing a dress that formed perfectly to her curvier, yet slender frame. *Damn.* A million fantasies ran through my head with only a back view of her in her gorgeous, black satin Gucci dress; there was something about her that made me want to see more - somethin' that drew me right out of my careless, cocky demeanor and practically forced me to levitate towards her. Stef finally noticed I wasn't listening to a word she said, but as I took off for this breathtaking woman, now heading in the opposite direction in the restaurant, she was the only thing on my mind. I practically ran across the room faster than I had on the treadmill during my lunch break that day, trying not to look funny jogging in silk cream-colored dress pants, and letting Stephanie scream after me. Normally, if I had my assistant with me, I would've just let him walk up to the girl, inform her I was interested, and sit back and wait for my prize, but there was something so intoxicating about this woman - just somethin' special about her that got me out of my seat.

I finally caught up to her and caught her arm on the way to her table. What I had done was totally out of character, but for some reason, I just couldn't even think to care. "Excuse me, miss, I couldn't help but notice you were alone tonight and I..." It was a line I had used many times to get some of the sexiest women in the city, but when this one finally turned around, I was at a loss for words. *Oh my god...*

She turned to look at me with distant eyes and a face I hadn't seen in so long. She didn't say anything but every word was said through her eyes. I was frozen. *Should I turn around?...I can't believe...What did I just do?...*

"Hello, Thomas."

*Damn. She beat me to the punch..What am I supposed to say to that?...She's not smiling or anything..just lookin' at me...*

Out of panic, I choked something out.
"He...Hi...'Ri...Marissa. How are you?" I couldn't believe it was her. Our eyes were locked and I was stunned and totally surprised and babblin' like a three-eyed fool. It had been years and she still had that *same* look that did the *same* thing to me. I couldn't tell what was going through her head. She just looked stern and serious, but so beautiful – more beautiful than she had ever been; her body was perfect and she had really grown up. She was a gorgeous, grown woman from head to toe. It had been so long.

"I'm fine. Just enjoying a night out; and yourself?" She just stood there in all her glory. I was a little aggravated, because she seemed to be completely in control of the situation; she had me wrapped around her finger, as usual. I wanted to turn around and leave her standing there so badly, to be furious at her for how she had treated me – the phone call to her mother's house a few years ago – but I couldn't. My cockiness and proud air flew out the windows of the restaurant and I stayed; I always had a sweet spot for that girl.

"Oh...I'm..I'm good...Uh...Hey, what are you doing down here?" I tried not to seem desperate but I'm not sure if I was successful or not. *Damn, why does she have to be so gorgeous?*

"I live here, Thomas. I just moved down here last year, after I graduated Harvard; I was on an accelerated program." She sat down at her table, crossed her legs and sipped her water.

*Yes!* "That's nice...do you work down here?"

She giggled and remained coy; she was desperately playing hard to get and it was starting to turn me on. I think she knew I wanted to know everything, but I was holding back to keep from seeming desperate. "I'm a corporate litigator for Dotson and Campbell." I always knew she would be somebody, so that was no surprise; it was the most prestigious firm in all of Miami and it suited her.

I couldn't stop staring at her and I really didn't know what else to say. I was already out of my element coming over there and because I chose to stay, a million questions raced through my head. All the memories came flooding back. The new me didn't want to care, but I still couldn't help but wonder how she felt after all those years, why we stopped talking completely, how she had been, what all she had been doing since graduation. Our eyes locked again and I thought I saw something there. "Marissa, I..."

"Hey, you; I thought you had left. I've been looking all over for you." Suddenly I heard a voice behind me and Stephanie popped up beside me. I had completely forgotten I had even been there with her and at first, her voice annoyed me for interrupting, but then I decided it was a close one. If she hadn't popped up, I probably would have told Marissa I missed her and suddenly, I didn't want to do that; that wasn't a part of the new me, so I snapped out of it.

"I'm sorry, sexy. Marissa, this is my date, Stephanie; Stephanie, this is Marissa." I intentionally left out that she was an old friend.

Marissa only looked at me for a second longer and turned to Stephanie with a fake smile. "Hello, Stephanie, it's nice to meet you." Then, the unthinkable happened; a tall guy was heading towards the table. "And here comes my date, as well."

I became instantly jealous. *Nice one, 'Rissa.* I made up some lame excuse of why me and Stef had to leave and hurried to get away, trying so hard not to look back. I just held her face in my head for the rest of the evening with Stef. I actually ended up taking Stephanie home and I didn't spend the night with her; instead I spent all night thinking about running into Marissa, how much it hurt that the visit was so short (I would have never imagined that that was how it would turn out, after all that time), how stupid I was, and wondering if I would ever even see her again...*I should've just told her I missed her....*

The next few days at work were pretty hard. I couldn't concentrate on cover-spread knock-outs with Marissa on my mind. It was so shocking for me to see her again and I couldn't believe I had wasted the opportunity, trying to be a big shot, actin' like I didn't care. She looked so beautiful, and I didn't look at her like a friend when I saw her. I realized, during that week, that maybe I was actually attracted to her. *Is this serious? Me...attracted to Marissa...my best friend...or ex-best friend...What the hell am I doing? She doesn't matter to me! She left me out to dry when I needed her the most! But I still miss her.*

279

My buddies at work started to tease me after a while; they said I
was fallin' off my game and that I looked like a lovesick puppy. I
just laughed off their jokes, trying to assure them that they
were wrong, but after two weeks passed since I saw Marissa at
the restaurant, I knew the only person I was fooling was myself.
I knew that for sure when I found myself dialing the operator
one Friday night, when I was supposed to be out with this
bombshell ex-porn star; instead, I was at home, praying that
Marissa Hall was in the telephone directory. I guess my swag
was slippin' again.

I jumped off the couch in joy when the operator said she
had the number and my maid looked at me like I was crazy; I
just shooed her away and tried to regain my composure as I
jotted the number down so quick I thought I was gonna break
the pen. *I hope she picks up. I gotta regain my cool, though.* My
heart beat skyrocketed as I waited for her to pick up, feeling
like I was in high school again. But when she didn't answer, I
wasn't too disappointed; it *was* her house number and I figured
she was working late. *What do I say now?* The tone sounded and
I had to think fast. "He...Hey, Marissa; this is Thomas
Barnett...Um...Our little visit the other night seemed a little
too short for my taste, so I figured you might want to meet for
drinks or..uh..dinner sometime this weekend. How about
tomorrow night...at Quinn's again? 7:30. Think about it." I
didn't know what else to say and I already felt like an idiot, so I
just slammed the phone down and ran my hands from the top
of my forehead to my chin and sighed. *What am I doing?*

Normally, I would have a few interviews with potential
Sweat models lined up for me to take care of on Saturday, but I
assigned them to my assistant and took the day off. I wouldn't
admit it to anyone then, but I spent the day hoping Marissa
would show up for our little date and picking out a new outfit
for the occasion. I was at Jos. A. Bank when it all caught up to
me and I realized what I was doing, but for some odd reason, I

didn't really care; I just wanted to take a chance. I figured it wouldn't cramp my style too much to let my guards down for an "old friend." *After all, it's just dinner...*

It didn't really feel like it was "just dinner" waiting for her to show up that night; I was nervous as hell, sitting there waiting for her and I felt like a loser for it. I was dressed impeccably in my new silk shirt and linen pants and I would never tell a soul that I was startin' to sweat a little; it didn't really help that she was late either - a whole hour late - and then my thoughts shifted. *I can't believe it - Thomas Barnett stood up by some old flame! Not even an old flame...my ex-friend! I don't have to take this, hell!* But as soon as I got ready to get up and leave, there she was – a vision in a flowing Versace dress, her hair pinned up and heels that accented her perfectly, sculpted legs. She *knew* she looked good and she had dressed that way on purpose. *Same old Marissa...*

I was so stuck on her that it took me a full sixty seconds of her standing right in front of me, for me to actually stand up and greet her, which wasn't very successful 'cause I didn't know whether to hug her or not. I did an awkward half-hand-shake-hug-thing and then remembered to say, "Hey, 'Ris...Marissa."

"Hi, Tom." She was in control *again.* "I happen to like my nick name, you know." She caught me off guard, as the waiter brought us water. I didn't know what to say again, for a moment, so I just apologized for not calling her 'Rissa before she went on. *Man, why does she have such a hold on me?* "You didn't think I was gonna show, did you?" She sipped her water, looking so breath-taking; I felt weird, because I felt myself just wanting to sweep her up in my arms and carry her home. *This is 'Rissa we're talking about!...Marissa Hall, best buddy, childhood friend..just friends!...You remember her, right?...Oooh, but her legs are so delicious.*

"Uh...I figured you were just busy with your makeup or somethin'." I tried to play it cool.

"Oh my God! Same old Thomas! C'mon, Tom; you know the way you acted the other night and that message you left on my voicemail was ridiculous!" She wasn't mad, but like I said, she saw right through me.

I didn't really know what to say; she had me cornered and it angered me but it reminded me of old times. *Should I just tell her how I feel?...Hell, I'm confused. It's been a while, but you know what!* "How do you expect for me to be, 'Rissa!" I got a little ticked, as we both shooed away the waiter.

"What do you mean?"

I didn't want to pretend anymore. "Oh c'mon, girl! Don't sit there and act like seven years ago didn't happen! You know what's up..."

"No, Thomas, I really don't. I know you changed; you've come to Miami and turned into a monster, even worse than you were in high school!"

We were a little loud, but we were outside on the patio and I didn't care; it was all coming out. "A monster! That's what you think I was..."
"I didn't have to think anything, Thomas; it was all coming to the surface – just one bad choice after the next." She was even gorgeous when she was mad.

"How could you blame me, after how you turned your back on me, 'Rissa?"

She gasped but then laughed hysterically. "Wow, Thomas, you really *have* gotten worse! Goodnight!" She got up and my heart jumped a bit. *No, don't' go!...I can't do this again...But I can't let her see me down...I just CAN'T!...* So, I just grabbed her arm, forcefully with a tight grip. The force of my jerk spun her back around and she stared at me long and hard, before she said, "I didn't come here to argue, Thomas."

My eyes pressed into hers and I didn't' loosen up. "Neither did I."

She stood there staring at me for a moment longer, before she decided to neatly sit back in her seat. I don't know if she could see the pleading cry in my eyes, because I didn't want her to, but she stayed. And after a long silence, she took a deep breath and went on. "Do you know why I wouldn't talk to you, after graduation - why I never came to see you for your birthday and I never wrote you all those years?"

*No, I don't! Care to explain why you broke my heart and deserted me like my...*"No, I do not."

"It's because you didn't realize that when you hurt Danielle, when you broke her trust in you, and sabotaged all you two shared, you did the same to me.." I started to talk but she cut me off. "...When I found out that you cheated on her at that party, Thomas, I didn't want to believe it. I kicked and I screamed and I hoped you didn't do it, but it was true and that hurt me. I was so depressed. I trusted you, Thomas, and I was hoping just as much as you were that you would never do anything like what you did - that your flirting would really be *just flirting* and that would be it. I put so much faith in you and you just ruined everything. I couldn't find it in my heart to forgive you at the time, so I just stayed away. You say I walked out on you, that I left you, but I felt like you betrayed me, when you

283

made the decision to sleep with that girl, because as a woman, I believe that if you will lie and cheat to another woman, you will lie to me. In the end, I felt like you walked out on me."

It was silent for a minute and I was so mad; I just wanted to say something to make myself feel like I didn't have to feel defeated, but I couldn't. There was really *nothing* for me to say. At least I had closure. "I never meant for that to happen, 'Rissa." That was all I could think to say to her, after all that had happened - after all those years of becoming "the new me" and after experiencing what I had experienced.

"Neither did I, Thomas; it's been hard these past few years without you."

*Really? That feels so good to hear from you.* The words felt so good on my ears and I wished I could tell her how good it made me feel to hear her say that, but I couldn't. "You have no idea how badly I wanted to be there for you with all that had happened, but you had hurt me so badly I just couldn't bring myself to do it – not after what you had done. It's been really hard." She looked into my eyes with her brownish gray ones and I wanted to leap across the table and take her into my arms but I concealed how I felt, no matter how hard it was.

"A lot has happened…but I was hoping we could move on." I said pointedly, while thinking: *Oh God, I missed you so much.* "…Maybe there's still a chance, beautiful."

She reminded me so much of my mother, as she tried to hide her smile. She tried so hard to be mad at me, just like when we were kids, but she couldn't, so we said "cheers" on the idea and went on with the evening, which ended up being pretty nice. We caught up on a lot of things from there and even though I was being really reserved about my true feelings, one thing was for sure: I was definitely attracted to Marissa as more than a friend. By the time I got home, I had convinced myself that it was okay, but I still felt awkward – even more awkward than I did when we had to say goodbye at the restaurant. I couldn't believe a part of me actually wanted to kiss her goodbye. I ended up giving her a hug - a long-awaited and long-lasting hug, after begging her to let me see her again. Again, I was acting "out of character" but what can I say - I'm only a man. She told me she would think about it, tryna be a tease, again, but I knew she would let me and she did.

After days of thinking about her, I got to take her out to dinner again and that night was better than the last; we had so many dates during the next few weeks that I didn't have time to date other women, even if I'd wanted to. My phone was ringin' off the hook from an amount of women in the double digits, but when I came home from being with Marissa, as much as I wanted to continue to sleep around, I couldn't. I was thinking about it one Saturday night after blowing off more potential models for the company to be with her, being scrutinized at work for it, and having my maid giggle every time she walked past me (she hadn't had to show a woman out, in the morning, for weeks)....*Man, I can't believe this...I never felt this way about 'Rissa before...I actually...This is totally not good for my image but, I actually... like her....*

The following Monday, I took her to a movie and it was so hard for me not to tell her how I felt. I didn't want to take that chance of putting myself out there, but she knew somethin' was up by the time we walked out of the theatre. "Why the long face, Mr. Big Shot?" (That was the nickname she gave me for being a famous gigolo and bachelor. She didn't agree with it – she fussed at me all the time for it – but she learned to get over it and accept me how I was.) "You cancel a date to be with me, tonight?"

"If I did, it's 'cause I wanted to." It slipped out. *Damn.
HOW DOES SHE DO THAT? It's just cause she looks so pretty...as
usual...and Oh God.*

We had made it outside and she suddenly stopped
walking. Her eyes sparkled in the bright lights of the theatre
and her face suddenly became serious. *Oh damn, here it comes.*

"What is that supposed to mean, Thomas?"

She was just so beautiful, and suddenly I couldn't control
my feelings for her. I had never looked at her like that before,
or I didn't think I did.

I paused for a while and looked into her eyes. *I can't.*
"You *know* how I feel about you, Marissa." I wasn't going to
open up to her too much – not even for a million dollars - and I
was determined to keep it that way. But honestly, I was secretly
praying she understood what I meant.

"I'm so glad, because I feel the exact same way." I was so
relieved that she understood; I took her into my arms, as her
car pulled up but suddenly I levitated towards her face with my
own. That time, I didn't even need to hesitate or ask one
question; I kissed her for the first time in my life - not on the
cheek like she might have done me when we were truly "just
friends," but - right on her gorgeous lips.

"Goodnight, Thomas." She got in her car and I just stood
there, breathless, as her car sped down the street.

*Wow.*

I figured out that that "wow" meant a lot of things that *I* didn't even understand, yet. I couldn't concentrate at work anymore and I had to practically force myself to look at other women. My co-workers made jokes about me on a daily basis and I just couldn't stop thinking about 'Rissa. And when I wasn't thinking about her, I was with her. The next few months flew by with the blink of an eye and I hardly had time to think about what was happening. *What am I doing? Thomas, wake up!* I was thinking at my desk one day, after hanging up with her. I had just called her at work to say hello and see how she was doing, that day. *Just calling to say hi? YOU DON'T CALL WOMEN, THOMAS; YOU FLAUNT THEM! What's wrong with me? I haven't felt this way about a girl since...Danielle... But it kinda feels....good. But no, no, no, no, no! I'm a bachelor! SOLO! I'm Thomas Barnett! Every woman wants me; why settle on one! But I can't stay away...I like her....*

It was getting harder for me to deny my feelings, especially seeing how no matter how much I tried to stay away from her, we went on more dates. We never asked each other anything about "boyfriend and girlfriend" and I liked it that way; I felt that if the subject came up, it would only complicate things more than they already were. I was so confused...I was really beginning to...like this girl a lot, but I wasn't sure if I was ready to give up my lifestyle for her...even though I desperately wanted to see what it would be like. But then, I thought about the break-up with Danielle and how much that hurt, no matter how much I tried to conceal it. I didn't know if I could go there again, but the next thing I knew, I had been dating Marissa for five months, my maid was getting used to seeing her around the house, my assistant started to hold any calls from old or new flames or potential dates, and I wasn't even getting mad about any of it.

*WHAT IS THIS, MAN!* I would ask myself over and over again, as I looked into her eyes across the table at dinner some nights or when we watched movies just the two of us, at her place or mine. I was ....scared...confused about myself - quite a few things, so I just stopped calling her. I told everyone to hold calls from her; I needed time to think and I didn't want to see her because when I was with her, I couldn't think, not about anything except how much I enjoyed being around her or how beautiful she was or how much she had always been there for me since we were kids or how genuine and sincere and just...EVERYTHING she was. So I just cut her off. It took me a week just to consider going on a date with a new girl and it wouldn't help when my maid would cut me dirty looks every now and then. I finally went out with some girl named Tiffany - another Ford model - but when I got back home from the evening at nine o'clock, I knew it was hopeless – that I was not gonna be able to date anyone except Marissa; I was hooked.

*What did I allow myself to get into? What the hell am I supposed to do, now? Just sit around obsessing about this chick all day and night...I can't do this anymore! I tried this before and it crashed and burned...And I can't even tell her how I feel.. How I feel! How the hell do I feel? What the hell is this that I'm feeling, anyways!* The maid let out a loud "Yes!" as I was cramped between the cushions of the couch sighing and holding my head between sippin' a glass of Scotch. She was just glad I wasn't out with some new girl. I cut her a dirty look and she disappeared into another room. Then, the doorbell rang and I started not to get it, but I figured what the hell, who could it be...can't get any worse than this. But I was so wrong.

"Guess I caught you off guard, huh?" She must've just gotten off work 'cause she still had her suit on and she looked so good. My heart jumped and I felt like a kid caught in the candy jar. My eyes were just frozen on her.

"Hey, 'Rissa" was all I could say; I couldn't believe she had come to my house and she was right; I was caught *completely* off guard.

"Can I come in?" I felt like I would be letting an angry lioness into my home, but I went ahead and took a chance; as much as I wanted to, I couldn't say no.

We sat across from each other in the living room and I felt like an arrested criminal. I could feel my maid's eyes staring at us from behind a plant in the kitchen. But that was the last thing on my mind, as I uncomfortably tried to avoid Marissa's eyes, just wondering what she was going to say; I was so nervous...*I can't believe she's here right now! What do I say?*

"I didn't want to hold you up, Thomas; I just wanted to make sure you were okay. I haven't heard from you in a while"

*Nice one! But I know you're too smart for that, 'Rissa.* She was playin' a game of cat and mouse with me and she had the upper hand.

"I'm fine." I was caught between staring at my feet and glancing up at her, every so often.

"Are you actually going to sit across from me and lie like that?" Her tone was calm but I still felt pestered.

*Here we go.*

I suddenly stood up with an annoyed look. "Listen, Marissa, I don't wanna do this right now, okay? I'm not tryna argue with you, girl."

"Well, we don't have to argue, Thomas, if you just say what's on your mind, instead of avoiding me; I've been worried sick about you!" She stood up as well and countered my look with anger.

Even though she was mad, I felt myself wanting to leap across the living room, gather her into my arms, and swoop her up to my bedroom. Instead, I just took a deep breath and went on. "I don't want to talk about it." I was as stern as I could be and I didn't want to go any further.

"Fine." she grabbed her purse and headed to the door. "I won't make you."

"Marissa, just stop it, okay!"

"Stop, what, Thomas? You obviously have some type of issue with us getting close or whatever, so why don't I just spare the both of us and cut you a break?" She was almost to the door when she stopped and turned around. "You know what, Thomas? I really thought that you and I could have something or at least try, after all these years! I thought that maybe, since high school you had done a little growing up – that you were just the same old Thomas, who said one thing and thought another. I figured the way you acted since the voicemail on my phone was just you still having not recovered from what happened with your mother and Danielle and whatever else is going on in your head. But standing right in front of you tonight, I'm not sure anymore and to tell you the truth, I don't want to do deal with that!"

I let out a loud howl like a mad man and hit the wall. "I tried to you let you in, something I DON'T do for ANY woman in my life and I haven't done it for years. It's not my fault you don't understand! You just want me to pretend that all that's happened hasn't happened....I'm only a man, Marissa; what do you expect from me? My God, girl; you got a lot of nerve!"

"Well, I do apologize for thinking that a grown man doesn't shield himself from emotions and feelings that he is bound to have, anyways! How will you ever forgive me, Thomas!"

Her voice was at the level of my own, as she started to open the door but I was too furious, by then, to notice. *Why couldn't she have just left me alone? Is that so much to ask!*

"So you're just gonna walk out on me, again, Marissa! Is that how the story ends?"

Instantly she turned her face to me, as she swung the door open and her face looked too familiar to the time I tried to grab Danielle's arm in the hallway and she began to cry and scream at me, after she had slapped me in front of everyone. The only difference was that I didn't need to be slapped after Marissa said what she said next; the force of the blow was just the same. "I guess it does." She slammed the door and I didn't chase after her; I just let out a loud, bellowing yell that made the maid come from behind the plant and fly out one of the side doors to go home. I couldn't even be hurt and I definitely wasn't going to cry; it was happening again. *Just when I let some girl back into my circle!* I was more furious than I had been in a long time – everything I felt seemed to turn into pure, uncontrollable anger and rage and it only spiraled from there.

I almost broke the door off the hinges, slammin' it into the wall of my bedroom, after stomping all the way up the two flights of stairs it took to get there. I had to be just as mad as a man can get, as what had just happened seemed to replay in my head like a bad movie I paid fifteen bucks to see. I was throwin' darts at my dartboard so hard I thought I would break it, when I realized how quickly any ounce of disappointment I could have been feeling, just disappeared; all that was left was fury. Suddenly, everything felt like high school all over again, a period of time that I had tried so desperately, for **YEARS**, to forget or at least get passed. *And she comes in here for ten minutes and makes it all fresh again!*

I didn't wanna think about it. I threw one dart. The thoughts slowly eased into my mind – Danielle and the fight, Natasha, not being able to really talk to my dad, Marissa not being there during the most difficult period in my life: starting college, her mother hanging up on me because she was whispering for her to do so, in the background. *I can't believe her!...*I threw another one...*And I let you back in again and this is how you repay me! Where was she when I needed her? She was supposed to be my friend no matter what....*I accidentally put a hole in the wall with that one...*I just let her into my head; she had me feelin' like I was falling...*my heart beat started to raise...*No, it's not that! I would never allow it to be that! No way...*

My anger escalated to a point it had never been, before and I felt a migraine coming on and I had run out of darts. I heaved my fist into the wall, my face had turned beet red, and all the sudden there was a ball in my throat far stronger than the anger steaming throughout my body. I hadn't cried since I was a teenager and that made me even angrier that I was about to, 'cause I felt like a spineless punk! *What am I supposed to do, now!* "Mom! Where are you, now?"

Finally, I collapsed unto my knees and grabbed my head to try to stop the migraine; just as I felt the slightest urge to do anything more, I caught myself, got up off the floor and decided to go out for a drink. *Never again will I let a woman get me that close to doing that. Never again.*

Sitting at my desk, it was a whole day later and what had happened the night before was still on my mind. I practically drank myself into a coma until two in the morning, hoping that the gin, scotch, straight vodka, and whiskey would overflow out of the glass and carry all of my issues away, but it didn't and I still had to go to work the following morning. The stack of new model profiles on my desk, towering over my head didn't help either. With all that was on my mind, I almost blacked out looking at it and my hangover was killin' me. I decided to step outside on my balcony for some fresh air and I got lost in thought.

"Hey, lover boy, you ready to see some clients, now?" Derrick from down the hall came by at the wrong time and I almost snapped on 'em, but I decided to just not answer. "Whatever it is, King, this will make it better." He sat a folder next to me on the balcony and disappeared. I could not have cared less what was in there but I was at work, so I had to do something. Derrick had taken the liberty to start the hiring process for my new secretary. Apparently, my old one had quit over the weekend. *Great.*

It took me three more days and more thoughts of Marissa before I opened the folder again. It was Thursday and I had convinced myself that "I wasn't gonna let this chick get to me anymore; screw her – I'm still Thomas Barnett and nobody can change that, not even Marissa. I did my best." I skimmed through the folder when I first got to work and decided to give Alicia Perez a call back but I got myself into a little trouble, because when she showed up at 9:30, I had to turn away after shaking her hand so she wouldn't see my pants.

She was FINE. After doin' nothin' but stressing about Marissa, she was the perfect little Puerto Rican thing to get her off my mind, if only for a minute. But, I was still frazzled so I tried to be curt, told her to sit down and tried not to look at her

293

behind, when she turned to sit in my imported leather seat. She had on something a little too sexy for the workplace, but I had already decided to give her the job *before* she told me she had graduated Florida State Suma Kum Lati, that she typed seventy-three words per minute, and that she was Hugh Hefner's assistant for a few months before she moved to Miami for a "fresh start." I cut her a break 'cause her body was perfect and her lips were better than Angelina Jolie's.

"You start tomorrow; don't be late; always look good; be ready for whatever I ask." I looked her over one more time as we stood in front of the door together, as I was showing her out. "And just be you." I meant that in more ways than one and I guess she caught on. I could tell by the way she said "Yes, sir" and walked out the door. I just sighed and thought *Please don't get me into trouble, Ms. Perez.*

Thanksgiving came and went and I decided I didn't care. I sent my dad a card and I still hadn't heard from Marissa since our fight, so I figured Christmas would be the same. I would never lie and say that I didn't wonder about her – how she was doing, who she was dating – but I would never admit that I missed her. I wanted to call her and talk to her for the holidays so bad some nights I would sit by the phone and just stare at it, but I never did. *What am I supposed to say? It's all ruined; she doesn't understand, I can't make her understand...And I don't really want to...I didn't ask her to come into Quinn's, that night...She didn't ask me to come over to her either, but I wouldn't have if I had known it would cause all of this...But it's not hard enough without her to call her and take the chance of doing all of this over again.* Luckily, Alicia kept me too busy at the office to think about much else with her racy outfits and the cunning way she always found an excuse to bend over my desk for things; she always smelled good and made me forget what I was doing, every time. I made a note to tell her to stop doing it, but never did.

Before I knew it, Christmas was around the corner and I didn't want to go anywhere. I had a heap of Christmas presents sitting in my living room from random girls and people wanting to earn my time, and three dates lined up that I made random excuses not to go to. So, I spent my Christmas thinkin' about Marissa again, out on the beach, drinkin' Scotch, and not letting anyone see anything in my face. *I need to snap out of this.* I started to feel ridiculous for not havin' someone by my house or at least being at the club letting twenty floosies flash me for a two-second glance at 'em, but I just gave up on it all and went to sleep. *Oh well. There's still New Years to look forward to.*

And it came really quickly – quicker than I would've wished. I wish I had known what I know now, when I got up to go to work that day, but it *was* New Year's Eve and crazy things always happen.  The office was so full of chaos all day, but I was so focused on work, before I knew it, it was eight o'clock and I was the only one in the office; at least I thought I was.

"What are you still doing here?" All the lights were out in the office and I was trying to make the final decision for the new cover spread, as I stared off into the computer, but my attention was jerked away from that when Alicia stepped into my office. She had on a tight red shirt and a pencil skirt that made flames dance all around my head and I swallowed real hard as I tried to find the words to answer her question before I got too excited.

I cleared my throat, "Just working on the final spread decision for the cover, before tomorrow…"

She slowly walked over to my desk and looked down at me in the dark. "That's in a few hours, sir and I need a ride home." *C'mon! Give me a break, Alicia. Why didn't you drive to work – this ain't New York. But you look so good, tonight.*

"I'm surprised your boyfriend isn't picking you up for a big New Year's Eve party." It was the only thing I could think to say as I tried to keep my eyes focused on the screen, but I didn't even realize that I was really probing for an answer. *I'm treading on forbidden waters, now.*

"I can say the same for you." Our eyes suddenly met and all of a sudden I felt like there was something about her that I needed to stay away from - which was easier said than done. "Now, are you gonna live up to your reputation of a callous, conceited jerk or can you take me home before midnight, señor?" Her accent turned me on and I looked away for a second, before I answered.

*I really shouldn't be doing this.* I chuckled. "Sure. You've been pretty good to me, so I guess it wouldn't hurt." She just smiled in response, as we headed to the door.

On our way to her house, I felt I hadn't felt so tense around a girl since my first date and I couldn't figure out why, or maybe I just ignored the reason. Either way, I think she noticed, 'cause she started some random conversation about New Year's resolutions or something, but my mind was elsewhere. *Why do I feel guilty? I used to go on dates every night and not think twice about it...This is nothin'.* I was convincing myself, but then I got to her house way too fast and I was nervous again; it didn't show, but I was.

"Thank you, Mr. Barnett." She looked at me with her sexy cat eyes and I had to look away to keep from glancing at her chest.

"Call me Tom; we're not at the office."

She giggled. *Even her laugh is sexy!* "Okay, Tom, would you like to come in for a drink?"

*Hell yeah!* "Um...actually, I need to go ahead and get home, myself - gotta make sure the maid did her job, today." The maid never did her job, 'cause she was too busy bein' nosy; I just wanted to get her out of my car before I...*What am I saying? There is a beautiful, young, attractive, sexy female in my car, inviting me inside for a drink and I'm rejecting her.*

"I understand." She looked down and started to get out of the car; instantly, I felt bad and decided that I could at least grant her that. After all, it was New Year's Eve...

"Wait...uh, I forgot she called me earlier; I can have a couple shots, but then I really need to get home." Marissa flashed into my head for a moment, before Alicia smiled and then I thought about the last time we had seen each other and sped into Alicia's driveway. I needed something to keep Marissa off my mind until midnight. *I don't have to do anything; it's just a drink.*

I followed her into her house and I think I complimented her on how nice the house was, before I sat down, still nervous. *If I'm gonna be here, I gotta stop actin' like this, man.* "Hey, you got any good Vodka?" I knew that would fix me up real good and luckily she did. I sat on the couch and waited for it and soon she joined me. She sat across from me and crossed her legs after handin' me the Grey Goose. I watched her discreetly as she walked away from me and a part of me wanted to reach out and grab her.

"So what's the VP of Sweat doing spending New Year's Eve with a boring girl like me?"

*I don't know. I was hoping you could tell me.* "You're a lot of things, Alicia but you are definitely not boring." I took a stiff sip of my drink and felt myself begin to relax a little.

"I'm flattered." She sat her drink down and slipped off her shoes; that brought my attention to her legs and I knew she knew it. She was teasing me and I can't say I wasn't enjoying it. She paused for a moment, as if she was feeling me out – speculating, plotting; I had seen the face she was making too many times with the girls I had been with before and I knew what she wanted, but I never got up to leave. "You know, from here, you look a little stiff, boss." It was nine o'clock by then and I knew where she was going with that statement, so I asked her for another drink. She got it, but this time, she handed it to me from behind the couch and then I felt her hands on my neck.

*Oh hell – please stop...*"You don't have to do that, Alicia."

"Oh, c'mon, boss; it's the least I can do for you taking me home."

I shifted to the side after sitting my drink down, trying to avoid her hands. "It's okay, Alicia; I'm fine."

Then a slight annoyance sparked in her face and tone. "I thought you were single. What – am I not good enough for you?" Her accent came out as she got upset and I realized what I was doing.

*What am I doing? ...I don't know why I feel this way, but if I don't stop, she will...Will that be so bad?....Man, what am I saying? She's practically throwing herself at me; what is my problem?* I came to my senses....supposedly... "You know what, sweetie; I'm sorry. It's not you; it's me....it's just been uh...a rough couple of months."

She moved to where I had slid to on the couch and slid her hands to my chest this time and I let her. "I'm trying to help you with that, Tom." And then, she did the worst thing she could have; she leaned down to my ear and whispered, "Just relax"...and I did. I let everything go, sat back, and enjoyed my massage.

She had great hands and before I knew it, I looked up and it was ten o'clock and she had given me two more drinks, unbuttoned my shirt at the top, and was *still* giving me one of the best massages I had received in a while. I let go of everything and all I could focus on was her hands on my neck and shoulders, how good she looked, and all the things I wanted to do to her, by that point. Before I knew it, she stopped. *Wha..What happened?* But then I figured out just what was happening, when she stood in front of me with her blouse open.

"Would you like to return the favor?" My eyes were as big as the headlights on an eighteen-wheeler and I could barely control myself. I tried to look away, but....*Are those double D's?*

I couldn't hold back any longer; I could feel my body beginning to take over. "Why don't you come over here and see." I didn't know where the words had come from. She slowly walked over to me and I could feel myself treading forbidden grounds *again* but I got ahead of myself. She was easing her way into my lap and that's when it happened. I had flashbacks...*Natasha*...It was Ashley G's party all over again, but this time....*Marissa*...With a force that came from I don't know where, I pushed her out of my lap and yelled, "Where's the bathroom?"

299

"Wha...What is the problem, Tom?"

"Where is it!" she pointed down the hall and I took off full speed to it, not noticing anything around me. I slammed and locked the door behind me and looked into the mirror. "What is wrong with me? Wha...What am I doing?...Damn, wha....Why couldn't I just do it?" I said pacing back and forth. Then, I just plummeted onto the toilet with my hands over my face, totally distraught and confused. *Man, this is too hard!...Why do I feel so guilty?...Why...*

I stood up and looked at myself in the bathroom mirror again, but I noticed I wasn't the only one in there, as a figure appeared behind me. I almost ran out of there out of fright, but then I figured I was just drunk. Something told me I wasn't, though and all the sudden, I was on the brink of tears. It was my mom. I was speechless; my heart almost stopped.

"Hi, baby." Her voice sounded so angelic and I couldn't believe my eyes, so I turned around to face her, to see that it was all real. I stared into her face, looked into her eyes, and it was her...she was so beautiful. "What's wrong, sweetie; you weren't expecting me?"

I didn't know what to say. I just stared at her in amazement – scared, nervous....ashamed; it had been so long...I...

"I've been watching you, Thomas; I've been watching you for a long time and I don't like what I've seen..."

I suddenly caught my breath, fighting the ball in my throat; I was never ashamed to cry to her before, but it had been so long since I had even seen her, so I didn't know how to... "Where have you...why...?"

She placed her soft finger over my lips and looked into my eyes. One tear slipped out and it felt like a release. She caught it as it slid down my cheek and wiped it away. "What are you doing, Thomas?"

"I'm in here with you...oh, in there...I don't know, Mom, I..." I turned around and walked across the bathroom. I couldn't face her for that moment, but then she appeared in front of me.

"You can't hide from me, Thomas Barnett – just like you can't hide from all the other things you've done."

But then I felt a little angry, but it was the kind of anger that is spawned from hurt. "But you haven't been here, Mom; I needed you all this time and you were never here!"

"Don't you raise your voice at me, Charles!" She only called me by my middle name when she was truly upset. "I've been here, all along and you know that!"

"But..."

"Baby, I've always been here." she grabbed my face and looked directly into my eyes; her words touched me like the whisper of an angel.

All the years of hurt came flushing back, all the years without her. "Mom..." I whispered every word, "When you left, I didn't know what to do without you. Everything has been so hard. I couldn't talk to anybody. I couldn't feel anything...you don't understand...I felt deserted...I needed you..."

"No, *you* don't understand, Thomas. You never needed me. All this time, you've been mistaken. I told you that neither I, nor your father was going to be there for you forever – that you needed to make wise decisions and be responsible. When did you think I was talking about, Thomas? You are a grown man, whether you act like it or not and *now* is the time."

Her words took my breath away and she told me to take my time, but then I decided that I didn't want to answer. "Listen to me, baby. I may not be here, in the physical, but my words shall stand true." She lifted my chin before I lowered my head. "It is time for you to grow up, Thomas. No more excuses, no more facades, no more reasons for you not to be the man that you need to be. Being grown up is not just an age; it is a mind -set and a way of life. It's time for you to be a real man, Son. It's time..."

I looked into her eyes and then grabbed her so tightly – the way I had wanted to for all those years I had been without her. I held her with everything I had in my soul and everything I had been missing since the day she lay lifeless in that casket. I couldn't stop the tears from flowing any longer... "I love you, baby."

And then she was gone.

I stood in the bathroom for a little while longer, feeling bereft, trying to collect myself and bringing myself to accept what had just happened; it was hard, but I did my best. I was cleaning up my face when I looked at the clock; it was 11:20 and I had to go. I sped out of the bathroom and flew back to the living room.

"Thomas, are you okay!" Alicia screamed to me, as I fled to the door. I didn't even answer; I had to get to my car before it was too late. I was a man on a mission, driving the freeways, swerving in front of everyone doing less than seventy-five. I had to get there in time, before it was too late. All I could think of was what I was gonna say, when I got there. I was nervous but something told me that the trip wouldn't be for nothing when I reached 1441 Northwest 179<sup>th</sup> Street; at least, I was hoping and praying it wouldn't be.

I stood outside the house and took a deep breath, before I ran to the door; it was 11:39 and she answered as soon as I knocked. She had her nightgown on, her face damp with tears. I instantly hurt again, as I pictured her sitting in her living room, all alone, crying her eyes out while I was at my secretary's place tryin' to get laid. It hurt me so badly, as my mother's words rang in my head. She started to speak, but I placed my finger over her mouth and forced my way inside, shutting the door behind me.

"I don't have much time. Baby, I missed you so much these past few years. The day you walked away from me in that hallway all those years ago hurt more than Danielle breaking up with me and it hurt so much more being without you because of what I had done. I spent all those years thinking about you, feeling stupid for not calling and trying to cover it up with football and women and awards...and Sweat Magazine...and MVP...and "King"... It hurt me so badly when you didn't want to speak to me. When I found out you were going to college, I didn't know what to do with myself. I wanted to be mad. I tried to be, but it hurt, Marissa." She tried to cut me off, but I went on and I was definitely on the verge of losing it. "Marissa, you don't know how hard it was for me to be without my mother; when she died, I felt like I lost everything. Baby, I felt like she left me. I couldn't love anybody because she was my favorite woman and she meant the world to me...It was too hard for me to love. It hurt too much; that's why I flirted around school. That's why I never gave my heart to Danielle completely or told her how I really felt about her..."

303

A ball began to rise in my throat as tears cascaded from her beautiful eyes unto my hands that had her hands neatly tucked within them. "I think I loved her, Marissa, but I didn't know how to feel it so I definitely didn't know how to tell it....I was so stupid so I slept with Natasha; I didn't even like her that much...I was just a stupid fool. I almost slept with another woman, tonight, but I couldn't do it, baby; I couldn't stop thinkin' about you."

Occasionally, a tear would fall from my eyes as I babbled on. I was reaching my breaking point as I got down on my knees. "I couldn't talk to my dad, all those years ago and he made me feel bad for crying, so I kept it all in and I feel like if I hadn't I wouldn't have lost Danielle...And I wouldn't have cheated on her...and I wouldn't have lost you for all those years...and I feel so bad and I'm so sorry for cheating on her. I never meant to cheat on her...She was on top of me and I felt cornered and afraid of commitment...and I lost it..."

She tried to talk again but I couldn't take it; the tears were flowing from my eyes so quick and I just had to get it out... It all came out. "It hurts so bad to have kept this all inside and I'll be lost if I can't have you, baby. I've been in love with you forever, but I was only a boy and I didn't know what love was and even if I felt it, I didn't know how to give it to you, 'cause I was going through too much. But I love you, Marissa. I love you so much and I don't want to lose you. You've always been the most important girl in my life, other than my mother, but I wanted to be friends because I was afraid of how good it could have been, afraid that you would make me love you, afraid that you would make me trust you and give you all my heart. And all I had, when I felt I didn't have anything left, but now I feel so dumb. I can't lose another woman I love...I can't take it again...I wanna marry you...I'll do it to keep you to myself...to keep from losing you again...I can't lose you again, Marissa..I won't...I can't be without you..." I was sobbing at her feet by then, writhing and clutching on to her like a child. I just desperately wanted her to forgive me and I wanted her to love me...I was hoping she would love me back, 'cause I couldn't take it if she didn't.

Her tears fell on top of my head, just as fast as mine did at her feet, before she raised me back to eye level. "I love you, too, Thomas; I've always loved you." She was breathless and it was all done. I had finally gotten it all out. I kissed her with all I had to give, as the clock struck midnight and I felt the greatest relief I had experienced since my mother died.

I was free from all the pain...free to cry because I knew it was okay. I was free to love and understand what the word *really* meant. I was free from what others thought of me and whoever called me a punk because I loved my girl and I bought her flowers and called her at work just to see how she was doing...I was free from sleeping with women to hide how I felt about the one woman in my life that I really wanted to be with and had wanted all along...I was free to tell my father how I felt about the day my mother died and how I always wished he would open up to me because I needed to hear it; I needed a good example of what a father should be, what a man should be. I was free to love my mother whether she was with me on Earth or not. I was free to be who I really was and take responsibility over my life and my actions. I was free to respect the woman that I cared for, to treat her how a woman should be treated and act like I care when she cries - when she hurts - to show her that I understand what it's like to be hurt, because I have hurt before, because I was no longer "only a man." At the stroke of midnight, in the arms of the love of my life, I had become a **REAL** man.

Thank you so much for having me...

## About the Author

At the time this book was first completed, Brandalyn Gill was a fun-loving, ambitious, and adventurous sixteen-year-old sophomore in college, merely pursuing her dreams and praying every day that every one of them would come true. She is a Houston-born resident, who has a deep passion for the literary art and is thankful for all the joy and excitement it has brought her. She graduated from high school at fifteen years old and began attending college at Lone Star College until she transferred to the University of Houston to become a junior at seventeen. She works hard in all that she does with every moment of life she is granted. She thanks God, her father, her mother, her Grannie, her Aunt T, her Aunt D, her Grandpa Reginald, her God family, her real friends, her 'Momma T' and any other soul sent to touch her heart in some way, encourage her, educate her, or just to spend precious moments of their life with her. She hopes that you have enjoyed or will enjoy this book and allow it to only positively influence your life in some sort – that it inspires you to live your life to the fullest, accomplish every dream you set your heart to desire, and enjoy life as long as you are granted the inestimable opportunity to do so. She has nothing but love for all those who have stuck by her throughout the years; she has and will see to it that they will be greatly rewarded, many times over.